ALIEN DISCLOSURE

EXPERIENCERS EXPOSE REALITY

LON STRICKLER

BEYOND THE FRAY
Publishing

ISBN 13: 978-1-954528-09-3

Beyond The Fray Publishing, a division of Beyond The Fray, LLC, San Diego, CA

www.beyondthefraypublishing.com

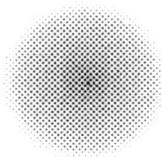

BEYOND THE FRAY

Publishing

Dedicated to those who know the truth.

ACKNOWLEDGMENTS

I want to thank the following friends and colleagues for their contributing research, investigations and assistance. They include, and are not limited to:

David Eckhart, members of Phantoms & Monsters Fortean Research (Butch Witkowski, Sean Forker, Timothy Renner, Tobias & Emily Wayland, Troy Noll, Rob Shaw, Brett Butler, Deleece Cook), Stan Gordon, Jamie Brian, Paul J. Lucas, Albert S. Rosales, Manuel Navarette, Ken Pfeifer, Matt R. as well as all the 'Phantoms & Monsters' readers.

Please be aware that a few of the eyewitness accounts in this book are written by ordinary people. Some text has been changed; but in some instances, it's been left unedited and as received. Thanks for your understanding.

Lon Strickler
McSherrystown, PA
www.phantomsandmonsters.com

INTRODUCTION

All of us have either stated or have heard the same questions concerning the actuality of alien beings. Who are they? What do they want? Where did they come from?

There are more theories than any person can shake a stick at. I suppose some hypotheses are more plausible than others, though most researchers tend to take a particular favorite position, and then discount other arguments. In the past, I have attempted to be flexible when it comes to the subject of alien beings; also referred to as non-terrestrials, extraterrestrial biological entities, ETs, etc. But my rationale began to solidify when I started to document the continuing incidents of otherworldly activity experienced by a family living in the panhandle of Florida, and subsequent experiencer encounters.

Around the same period of time that I had begun working with this particular family, I had also initiated a daily regime of training in order to become a capable remote viewer. Combined with my natural intuitive abilities, I would then soon realize a series of strange existences beyond our dimensional reality.

Since 2008, it had become increasingly apparent to me that

we are not alone as a single intelligent species in the cosmic ocean. But it has also become apparent that our Earth and overall humanity have attracted the attention of non-terrestrial beings over many millennia.

Why are these alien beings so concerned with Earth and its dominant human species? The most straightforward answer to that question is that we retain a connection to them.

After decades of research, investigation and personal experience, I believe that an early interaction between Earth's inhabitants and otherworldly beings occurred between the 13th and 12th millennia BCE. I don't sense that this was the first or only interchange, but I do consider it to be the most influential.

As the result of several remote viewing sessions and three personal non-terrestrial encounters (which includes a lost time event), an historical scenario was displayed to me. I witnessed a colossal disc-shaped craft descend and land in the area of the present-day Nile River delta. At that time, this location was completely encircled by the Mediterranean Sea, and that this craft was later transformed into a massive and magnificent island. This was the genesis of a great empire that encompassed the surrounding indigenous people and land. The rulers of this empire were the occupants of the craft that landed there. Their knowledge was disseminated throughout the region, and their bloodline was merged with the native people.

The aliens communicated to me that this empire was the nexus of several dominant and lesser civilizations. I asked them; "Was this Atlantis?" There was no response to my question. I witnessed representations of various cultures that developed over millennia. Some were brief glimpses of time while others were mighty empires. But all had a direct connection to the occupants of the craft.

There was particular emphasis made to the development of

the ancient Egyptians. I observed order created out of chaos; a civilization that was deeply influenced by the beliefs of the extraterrestrials. For thousands of years, there were continued interventions by the alien Gods.

I was presented with a particular series of events that occurred during Egypt's 18th Dynasty. This has been classified as the first dynasty of the New Kingdom of Egypt, an era in which ancient Egypt achieved the peak of its power. A profound encounter occurred during the reign of Amenhotep III, which greatly affected the royal family and the Priesthood. This encounter was interpreted by Amenhotep III as a divine message that the Pharaoh was a God that rivaled Amun-Ra and the Priesthood. Amenhotep III's display of power and distain for the Priesthood was watched closely by his son Amenhotep IV (who later changed his name to Akhenaten). When Akhenaten became Pharaoh, he established a quasi-monotheistic belief in the solar deity Aten, which I believe was a representation of an alien being or craft.

It is also my belief that his brother Prince Thutmose, who was earlier banished into the eastern desert for unknown reasons, later returned to Egypt during the early 19th Dynasty as the Hebrew prophet Moses.

What I observed over the years eventually altered my perception of human history; that our past is intertwined with extraterrestrial beings. Modern humans are a genetic extension of otherworldly species. I also believe that most of the alien entities that people encounter are biologically enhanced and evolved humans from our past and future.

But we must always keep in mind; they do have an agenda. I believe that agenda is eventual technological and biological singularity. My premise may become more apparent as you read this book. The experiences described in the accounts are brutally forthright. Some readers may be shocked by the details. But then again, I don't believe that you would want me to present the information in any manner that isn't consistent with the experiencers' actual encounters.

Lon Strickler

AFRAID OF THE DARK

"Disclosure: (n.) when they finally tell us everything and nothing changes."
- Sol Luckman, The Angel's Dictionary.

IT IS human nature to be fearful of the unknown. That being stated, many people are aware that there is more to our existence than what we see on Earth. We seek answers to questions about a higher intelligence beyond the bounds of this planet. In the course of these inquiries, we ask if the powers that be have secret knowledge of non-terrestrial races and technology. Eventually we wonder if official disclosure of the truth will ever be communicated to the populace. I truly doubt this will occur, unless an overwhelming incident leaves the government with no other choice. Then I expect that we would be spoon-fed information in order to calm the masses.

OK. I'm finished being cynical about government disclosure. But I do believe that experiencer disclosure and the evidence procured from their encounters offers us an actual sense of the truth.

Before I go any further, I want to include a brief statement about receiving witness information. I realized a long time ago that it's best to listen to what people tell you, make detailed notes along the way, and then compare the information with other reports and known facts. This also includes being open-minded and initially giving the experiencer the benefit of doubt. When asking questions, it's best to be brief in order to clarify their statement; otherwise, the witness may begin to include embellished information. After several decades of interviewing eyewitnesses, being able to separate the wheat from the chaff (or better yet, determining truth from bullshit) becomes second nature. I have learned that a high percentage of witnesses actually believed they had a remarkable sighting or an unexplained encounter. They took the time to trust you with their information, which is an important factor to consider.

Abduction and alien contact experiencer reports can quickly trigger skepticism with an investigator, especially if the information is received by telephone or in-person. The demeanor of the individual is usually full of fear, confusion and uncontrolled emotion. It's important to listen and avoid making instant judgements based on the first interaction. But sometimes you will receive a call in which you 'know' that something remarkable occurred in this person's life, and that you are now about to become a part of their story.

In July 2009, I received that call. A young woman, named Mandy, stated that her life had become a living Hell and that she could no longer leave the house in the evening. "I am literally afraid of the dark and under siege in my own home at night!"

Mandy was living in a farmhouse outside a small town in east-central Washington, less than a mile from the Idaho border. About two weeks prior to contacting me, her and her mother had noticed bright red and white lights hovering above the Coeur d'Alene Mountains. As they watched the lights, Mandy began to feel dizzy and fearful. That night, she had a horrific nightmare that involved constant flashing lights and loud mechanical noises. The next morning, she woke feeling nauseous and light-headed. Mandy was a school teacher but had to call in sick.

By the next day, Mandy began to feel better, but the lights over the mountains continued on for several nights. She no longer had any dreams, but she still had the sense of fear linger with her. Her mother thought that Mandy was simply over-reacting to the sighting of the lights.

Then a few nights later, Mandy and her mother were in the kitchen cleaning up after a late dinner. They began to hear popping sounds coming from the back yard. As they looked out the window, they both noticed hundreds of small red and white lights flying in all directions. Each time a pair of lights collided, there was a distinct popping. Mandy ran into the living room and looked out the window. There were red and white lights everywhere, out by the road and in the field.

Her mother picked up the telephone in order to call the police, but there was no dial tone. By that time, the lights in the house began to flicker. There were also strange sounds coming from the roof, similar to scratching. This continued for about 5 minutes, then suddenly stopped. They were both confused and scared. The phone was now working, but her mother thought that there was no reason to call the police.

Mandy walked outside to see if there was any indication of what had just occurred. Everything seemed fine, but there was a slight odor in the air. She told me that it reminded her of burnt motor oil, but she couldn't find a source. She eventually went back inside the house, but still bewildered by what had happened.

The next night, at approximately 10:30 p.m., Mandy was getting ready for bed. While standing in front of her bathroom mirror, she noticed two loud thuds on the roof. She went into her mother's room to see if she had heard the sounds, but she was already in bed asleep. While walking in the upstairs hallway towards her room, she heard several more thuds on the roof, as well as scampering sounds in the attic. She looked out her bedroom window and once again witnessed hundreds of small red and white lights flying about in different directions. The noises in the attic had waken her mother. They both yelled for each other, as all the electricity in the house cut off.

They ran into Mandy's room and sat nervously on the bed. The thuds on the roof and the scampering in the attic continued. They lit a few candles, hoping the activity would soon end. They felt like prisoners in their own home, worried about what would happen next. Then suddenly, the lights came back on and the noises stopped. Mandy later told me that the commotion went on for at least an hour. Neither of them got much sleep that night.

A few days later, Mandy contacted me by telephone. I was referred to her by a paranormal investigator in Spokane. As soon as I began talking to Mandy and her mother, I sensed that this was not any run-of-the-mill unexplained encounter. They had once again experienced similar activity the previous night. Mandy commented that she felt like they were both in danger and asked if I had ever heard of a similar experience. I was understandably dumbfounded by the series of events but, at the same time, I was concerned that the activity may eventually lead to a physical intervention. I didn't mention my unease.

I believe that we talked for about three hours. There was nothing exceptional about Mandy and her mother. They had lived together in the family home since Mandy was born. There was no information offered about Mandy's father, so I didn't press the issue. Her mother had recently retired from her position as a state worker. I asked them to keep a journal on the activity and to contact me. This is my normal routine when working cases. During the interview, Mandy asked; "Why is this happening to us?" I didn't want to tell her that they may have been singled out, but I really did sense that this may have been the case. Little did I know, it would be my last contact with Mandy.

After I got off the telephone with Mandy and her mother, I started to examine several incident databases in an attempt to find any similar events. Continued activity to the same witnesses over a period of time is somewhat unusual, and I was concerned that there may eventually be an escalation.

The next day I expected to receive a follow-up telephone call from Mandy. In fact, I called and left a message asking that she let me know if there had been any further activity. I waited for three days, and no telephone call or email came my way. Then, on a Sunday afternoon, the anticipated call came. It was Mandy's mother. She apologized for not getting back to me. There was an obvious distress in her voice. After a brief pause, she calmly said; "Mandy is missing."

I got a sudden sick feeling in my stomach. Mandy had gone to bed not long after we had talked on the telephone. Her mother remained downstairs in the living room watching television. At about 11 p.m. she decided to go to her bedroom. As she passed Mandy's bedroom, she noticed light coming from the bottom of the door. She knocked on the door in order to check on her. There was no response. As she opened the door, the room went completely dark. She flicked on the light switch by the door and observed that Mandy was not in bed. She called out to her, but there was no response. Panic was beginning to set in as she literally screamed, "Mandy!" while running throughout the house. There was no trace of her, inside or out. Mandy was gone. The local authorities had no explanation. All of Mandy's personal items, including her car, remained. It was as if she simply vanished. Since Mandy was an adult, there wasn't really much that the police investigators could do. They suspected that she took off with someone during the night. I asked her mother to keep me updated, but I never really expected to hear back from her. As far as I know, Mandy has never returned home. The last time I made an inquiry with the Washington State Police, her case remains unsolved.

Mandy's disappearance still haunts me. I am certain that she was abducted by an unknown force, but that doesn't absolve me of feeling a bit of guilt. I realize that my regret seems ridiculous since there was nothing that I could have done. Nonetheless, I suspect that the stigma of her ordeal will always remain with me.

2

THE ABDUCTION SCENARIO

HUMAN TECHNOLOGY HAS DRAMATICALLY EXPANDED in the past century. It's difficult to believe that there has not been some degree of support offered by a higher intelligence. But at what point did this intervention begin? Were the seeds of advanced science sown during early contact, and allowed to germinate at a specific pace? Was humankind then given a green light to accelerate their technological prowess during the twentieth century? How has this altered the human-alien connection?

In the past decade, there seems to be more diversity when it comes to alien contact with humans. A progression of advanced intelligence and technology by non-terrestrial beings has become more evident to experiencers. Abduction and close encounter descriptions are more complex and esoteric. Accounts of cloaking, portals, physical transformation and other extraordinary activities are becoming more apparent.

In the 1940s through the 1990s, an abduction scenario usually followed a similar process. Most times, the alien captors originated from a type of craft or UFO. After securing the human subject, they would return to the craft. The subject was rendered immobile by hypnosis or by an induction of a drug, then laid on a metallic table for examination. The alien captors would conduct a variety of tests and scans, which was usually followed by a collection of body fluids or tissue. On many occasions, these collections involved procuring sperm samples from a human male and embryos from a human female. After the examination and testing, the human subject would be shown images of the future of life on Earth. It was always a gloom and doom sequence of events; a warning that Earth was destined for destruction by our own hand, and that changes must soon begin.

But in some cases, a glimmer of hope would be introduced to the abductee. An image of a group of humans, performing every-day tasks, would be shown. A question was then asked to the subject, in essence; "Which of these people are not human?" The subject would look closely and then respond that all the people were human. Then a reply would follow; "You now see; this is the future and it will be good for all."

I was beginning to hear these suggestions of human-alien hybrids and integration being presented to abductees around the late 1990s. More and more female abductees were coming forward and talking about lost pregnancies after the first trimester. In other words, the female experiencer was abducted, and the fetus was removed. As well, male abductees were describing situations where they would 'meet' a hybrid child during their abduction, where it was obvious that this was his offspring.

The types of non-terrestrial races involved in these incidents was also evolving. Rarely were abductions only carried out by the 'Greys' and human-like hybrids. In recent years, we have interviewed abductees who have described upwards to 4-5 different types of beings carrying out various functions during the abduction event. What could be the reason behind these noticeable revisions in alien abductions? Are humans now being subjected to an intense 'redesign' by these captors, resulting in an integration of the species? Has alien artificial intelligence already become a distinct part of modern humans?

I stated in the introduction of this book that I was conscious of a single personal abduction, even though I am positive that there were other incidents. These personal incidents also include several close encounters. Alien abductions tend to be a long-term endeavor for the experiencer, resulting in multiple events over many years. As well, there is usually a history of alien contact and abductions with other generations of the family. In recent years, some researchers have claimed that a majority of experiencers did not have the Rh factor in their blood, and that most of these people had also possessed the O type. This may be true, but I believe that more research is needed before we can designate these elements as a distinction or reason to why certain individuals are chosen.

Most of the abduction scenarios I will present in this book occurred in the past twenty years. These accounts are from actual experiencers who came forward to me or my colleagues in order to ask questions and to find explanations. I don't pretend to have all the answers or assume to satisfy each person's expectations. I can offer my opinions and theories, and in certain cases I can provide additional help through remote viewing or my intuitive abilities. But the experiencer will eventually need to determine how they will come to terms with their ordeal.

———

THIS ACCOUNT WAS FORWARDED to me in 2010. Rosario's scenario is a bit scary and may verify some concerns involving alien intentions. In our conversation, Rosario seemed very sincere and demonstrated spontaneous emotion when certain subjects were discussed:

"I want to thank you for allowing me to tell my story. I have been a subscriber to your site for over a year and it has inspired me to open up so others be made aware of the complications that humans may face after an abduction by alien beings.

One early morning during the late summer of 1990, I awoke from a very deep sleep. It was 3:35 a.m. and still dark outside, though I'd be up in an hour or so since it was harvest time on the farm.

I was feeling nervous as my heart pounded heavily. I sensed that there was someone in my bedroom, but all I could see was a spot of light in the corner by the dresser. Suddenly several hands grabbed me from all around the bed. I attempted to scream but could not move or say anything, nothing came out of my mouth.

Within seconds I found myself lying on a cold hard table completely nude and terribly uncomfortable. I looked around me and there were four small beings in hoods and loose robes standing around me. They were conversing with each other, but I could not understand what they were saying since it sounded like a young child's gibberish. I felt something touching me all over my body but could see nothing. The beings' faces had a weird glow with sagging folds of shiny skin.

After what seemed like forever these beings slowly moved aside and this human-like man walked up to my side. He was tall, bald and had very pale skin. He also had large round eyes and was very slim. He came over to the table and started to talk to me in English. He calmly said that he was perplexed that I was so scared since he made it clear the last time that they had met he would return to ask a favor. He then turned and raised his hand, gesturing to a woman who walked into the room. She seemed to be a normal human female and quite beautiful. She had a small bundle in her arms and walked over to me. It was an infant, but it had pale skin and didn't look quite human.

The tall man instructed me that he wanted me to take the infant and care for it. It needed the love of a human mother since their race did not understand the emotion of love. I told him that I couldn't because I already had a child and it was hard enough raising my son alone on a farm when times were difficult for me. He raised his head up and down as if agreeing with what I said and passed his hands across my eyes. I must have passed out because I awoke in my bed.

It was daylight and I figured that I had been 'gone' for about five hours. When I tried to get out of bed, my legs and hips were very stiff and sore. I carefully stood up and noticed two large spots of wet blood on the bedsheets. The experience with the beings was still fresh in my mind but I had no idea that I had endured any probing or surgery.

A few days later, I decided to schedule a doctor's appointment just to make sure I was OK. The doctor recommended a full physical since my blood pressure was higher than usual and my ankles were swollen. An appointment was made at my local hospital for x-rays and blood work.

To make a long story short, I returned to my doctor's office a few days after the tests were performed. When I walked into her office, she asked me to sit down and explained that my right kidney was missing. She said that it was probably missing since birth and was just never noticed. I found this hard to believe since I had given birth to my child and have had other x-rays in the past. I just agreed with her assessment and was instructed that I would need to start taking *hypertension medication and would need to be regularly monitored.*

I am positive that the beings removed my kidney and performed other experiments on my body. Though it has been almost twenty years since that encounter, I just know that they will be back.

Lon, have you ever heard of organs and/or body parts being harvested from abducted humans?

I sincerely hope I can eventually get some answers."
Rosario - near Cody, WY

I did talk to Rosario and assured her that she wasn't the only person that I knew of who had whole or parts of organs removed 20 during an abduction or encounter. It's been about a decade since I last talked to Rosario for an update. I hope she found some solace.

———

I RECEIVED the following account in December 2016, from an experiencer in Columbus, Ohio:

"In the early morning of Nov 11th, I had suddenly awakened feeling afraid and aware that something was wrong. I abruptly witnessed three creatures leaning over me. I attempted to reach my nightstand to grab my .38 but as soon as I moved one the creatures pointed some sort of small light at me. There was a buzzing and I was suddenly paralyzed. My wife was still sleeping, but I was unable to look at her.

The next thing that I remember was laying naked on a cold metal surface. The creatures were transporting me through a bizarre hallway; grayish walls with a reptile scale texture to it. It was very warm and moist and had a sickening 'fishy' odor. The hallway was very bright. I could start to move, but my body was stuck to the metal surface.

We briefly stopped moving and I was able to glance into a lighted room on my right. There were several of these creatures examining a large floating square with a digital map of the Earth that was turning. There were lighted 'targets' on the map, which seemed to designate positions of cities. There was another taller creature among them, but I didn't get a good look at it.

I was soon being moved to any well-lit and very loud room. It sounded like a huge ventilation fan was running, though I didn't see anything. One of the creatures waved it's four-fingered hand over my face. As soon as that happened, I went completely numb. I could still see, even though I felt drowsy and could not speak. A long metal tube was inserted deep into my nose and sinuses, and soon a similar shaped tube was inserted into my mouth, reaching far back into my throat. I started to gag, and it was quickly removed. They wrapped several narrow bands around my limbs and torso. They were also removing samples of tissue and hair, but I only felt pressure while this occurred. After that, everything was a blur; though I remember waking in my bed and looking at my clock. It was 5:37 a.m. My body ached all over. I attempted to wake my wife, but she was totally non-responsive. I believe that she had been drugged. I wondered what the hell happened to me. I got up and walked to the bathroom. There were no wounds, but I was terribly sore in my groin and neck.

The creatures (I don't know what else to call them) stood about five foot tall and wore no clothes. Their bodies had no sexual features and the arms very long. Their skin was a greenish-gray color and hairless. Their heads were large and turnip-shaped, with large almond-shaped black eyes. No ears, just a small hole on each side of their heads. There were *nostrils, but more like a pair of nickel-sized orifices. Their mouths were small, that I never saw open.*

I have never believed in this type of thing, and I still wonder what this was. I don't want to think 'alien abduction,' but that is why I am writing you. Is this what happened to me? I was raised in a Christian order that teaches us that aliens and the supernatural do not exist. I still believe this, but now I'm questioning my upbringing. What else could it have been?" HJ

Most abduction scenarios are fairly similar in description. It could be that people are coming in contact with the same beings or that the entertainment media has tainted experiencers' psyche. This witness, like many others I have interviewed, definitely believes that they had an extraordinary encounter. The religious factor in this situation is a bit different, since it is an obscure sect.

The witness told me that he has never had anything similar happen to him and is afraid that another encounter may be in his future. He is worried that his wife and children may endure the same procedures. He has no proof that this will happen, but like most abductees, there is a sixth sense about these matters; which usually comes to fruition.

———

THE NEXT ACCOUNT was forwarded to me in November 2016:

"I was in the US Air Force (1962-1970) and volunteered to go to Vietnam in 1965. I got orders to go to Nha Trang but when I arrived in Saigon, I was instead sent to Thailand and ended up at Udorn RTAFB which in the north close to the border of

Laos. It was a small base with just a couple of hundred personnel. We didn't even have any jets, just prop planes.

A couple of months after my arrival, the base started really ramping up. They built a whole new barracks area and more personnel started arriving. I was an electronics technician in the Communications Service. We had a tiny Comm Center next to the runway. There were 4 vans with crypto gear parked next to each other with a Quonset hut for the teletype machines centered on the vans. There was a hooch we used as the shop and a couple of others for the radios and other comm equipment. We had wooden pallets laid out for sidewalks, as it got pretty muddy during monsoon season. At the end of one walkway we had a water buffalo, a big water tank on wheels that held our drinking water.

During night shift, it was the newest guy's job to make coffee for everyone in a big urn. You'd carry the urn out to the water buffalo, fill it, bring it back and do your thing. So, one night (this had to be in early 1967 as we were already living in the new barracks but the new comm center wasn't completed yet) the new guy hauled the urn out to make coffee. After a while, somebody noticed he hadn't returned and went looking for him. He found the urn laying on the ground by the water buffalo but no sign of the airman.

We went on alert; the base was locked down and a big search started. He was gone! Naturally, we all assumed he had been snatched by the Pathet Lao, Laos' version of the Viet Cong. What we couldn't figure out was how they could have penetrated into the center of the base. And why grab an 18-year-old Airman 3rd Class teletype operator? Due to the treaty with Thailand, we couldn't carry weapons, so it was up to the Air Police to tighten up security. We were pretty spooked. It was probably a good thing we didn't have guns!

Three days later I was in my hooch and a guy came

running in saying they found the missing guy! They found him on the ground right next to the water buffalo! Now, the missing guy's hooch was right next to ours, so I went in there. A minute later he came in, escorted by an AP, and started grabbing his stuff and throwing it in his duffle bag. I asked him what had happened, and he said, "I've been ordered not to talk about it." I asked him where he was going and he said; "To Japan." The AP was very uncomfortable and told me not to talk to him, so I shut up. I looked him over as he packed and could see he was in fine shape. He was clean, but I noticed there were three or four deep scoop marks on his cheek.

He finished up, said goodbye and off they went. We never saw him again and I never heard anything else about the matter. We all shrugged our shoulders and figured the Pathet Lao weren't the type that beat up their captives. We couldn't figure how they penetrated the base twice though. We figured it was just to intimidate us and things just went back to normal. I was happy when we got moved into the new Comm Center and away from that spooky spot by the runway.

Years later, in the 1990s, I was watching a TV show about alien abductions and they said something about the victims having skin samples scooped out of their cheeks. I suddenly flashed back to that event and remembered the marks on that airman's face. Could it have been?" GF

Could this incident have been an actual alien abduction? If it was, it wouldn't have been the first time an abductee was assumed to have been returned several days later.

A LONGTIME READER forwarded the following NUFORC account; apparently because the people involved in the incident were acquaintances of the reader and that they were well-aware of the circumstances:

> "At approximately 1:15 AM on 11/20/04 my wife and I retired to sleep on the second level of our Boca Raton, FL home after watching TV in our first-floor den. As I often do, I put on our TV in our room which helps me to get to sleep. As I watched a National Geographic special, I became groggy. Knowing that keeping the TV on all night bothers my wife, I grabbed the remote and switched off the TV and quickly fell into a deep sleep. In what seemed an instant after doing so, I was awakened by my wife who questioned me as to where I was. My immediate response was; "in our bed."
>
> My wife then explained to me that she awoke because she sensed that I was not in bed with her. She then stated that she searched the whole house and even walked to the community guard house in her pajamas to see if anybody had been permitted to drive to our residence to pick me up. She was told nobody had come into the community.
>
> Upon her return, she burst into the room and found me in our bed. She stated that my car was in our driveway, and that my wallet, cell phone and money was just as I had left it in our kitchen when we went upstairs, which further upset her. She knows me well enough to know that if, in fact, I left our home for some reason, I would have taken these items with me. We do not live near any stores or establishments that one could walk to.
>
> As I awoke, she further explained that the covers in our bed on my side looked exactly as if I had pushed them down and left the bed. Realizing that she was not kidding, I informed her that I just turned off the TV and fell asleep. She then reconfirmed that she searched our entire residence and that I was not physically present.

I glanced at the clock and it was about 2:30 a.m. when she stormed into our bedroom and awoke me with this shocking news. I tried to comfort and console her at this point and confirmed that to my knowledge I had not left our bed, not even to use the bathroom.

Not really sure what had happened, we went back to bed. When I awoke, I asked her to confirm what had happened and that either her nor I were dreaming. She confirmed it.

Somehow, I do not think either of us actually accepted this event as reality because we awoke and did not talk about it. As a believer, I felt that I needed to let somebody know and help me to understand what might have happened. I searched the web and found this site to report incidents. I called and was instructed to file this report as I am.

I consider myself of sane and sound mind and am a local business owner. I was also instructed to have my wife file an incident report which will be done first in the a.m. I am also willing to have this event scrutinized by any means required to validate it, including an on-site investigation, cameras, lie detectors, etc.

It almost seems like something out of the 'Twilight Zone' and I feel more confused than anything. I am not sure what really happened. The evidence has it that I was somehow physically missing from my home for 45-60 minutes without my knowledge.

I was told to examine myself for any marks and did not find any. However, from the base of my throat to the middle of my chest it is mildly red, as if I had been exposed to the sun. I can tell because when I press the area, a brief mark appears such as when one gets a sunburn and presses the affected area with a finger. The rest of my body is unaffected."

The reader (KL), who forwarded this report to me, stated

that he believes the incident actually occurred. MUFON and NUFORC both made inquiries. NUFORC was under the impression that this was a hoax, which is a consistent reaction by the group when a witness goes silent. According to KL, the experiencer had a 'visit' from a government agent no more than thirty-six hours after the incident. The experiencer and his wife became extremely upset by the visit and refused to continue cooperating with the reporting agencies. The couple had a number of unexplained 'encounters' over the next three years. They moved to another location and never contacted KL again. KL believes the couple have since passed away, according to inquiries that were made in 2015.

———

I RECEIVED the following account in July 2017:

> *"Hello Sir, the information I am about to disclose to you can be published, but my identity and personal data must be kept anonymous. You may contact me through my email, if you have further questions. I will begin by stating that I am a public servant in the American political establishment. Because this story is a sensitive issue to me and my family, I ask you to be discreet. I have been a subscriber to your publication for several years and I am confident that we can trust you. I hope our story will benefit your continued research.*
>
> *In the spring of 1996, my wife and I were newlyweds and we were living in a townhouse in my hometown. One night, we had just gone to bed, approximately 10:45 p.m. After lying in bed for a few minutes, I heard an odd 'humming' coming from the upstairs hallway. I asked my wife if she heard it, and she acknowledged that she had. When we looked towards the*

open bedroom door, the hallway started to lighten with a blue hue. As we watched, the bedroom door began to close. Then a large oval-shaped blue light appeared on the bedroom wall near me. At that point, we both must have gone unconscious. This is the last we remember of any activity in the bedroom.

The next moment that I remember was becoming conscious but feeling dull pain throughout my body. I was lying flat on my back on a table of some sort, and as I looked around, I couldn't distinguish anything other than a faint blue light filling a large room. I immediately began to worry about my wife. I started to yell out but was quickly silenced by something placed in and over my mouth. My head was then secured and immobile. I could not see anyone or anything around me, but I was having difficulty breathing and soon blacked out.

I once again became conscious, but this time I was on my back in a reclining chair. I was strapped in, but able to move my head. Again, I didn't see anyone or anything. My mouth and tongue were numb and the only sounds I could utter were moans. I have no idea how much time was spent in the reclining chair, but it seemed like many hours. I was deeply concerned about my wife's status and what was happening to me. The room was somewhat smaller than the previous room and barely lit. I must have fallen asleep, because the next moment I remember was waking and seeing three tall, lanky beings standing around the chair.

These beings must have been seven-eight feet in height and were very thin in the body, with long thin legs and arms. The hands had four long fingers with no nails. Their heads were about the size of an adult human but similar in shape to the Grey aliens normally seen in your newsletter. They had the same large black almond-shaped eyes and their coloring was very pale. They were wearing a light blue spandex-like material that covered the body, arms and legs. I also noticed an odor while in their presence, similar to strong garlic.

The chair reclined and I was once again flat on my back. One of the beings was looking through a device that was suspended over my groin. I felt intermittent stabbing pain in my testicles during the examination. This continued for a few minutes. Then another being place a plastic-like covering over my face. That is the last moment I remember in the presence of the beings.

The next moment I remember after this ordeal, was me waking in my bed at home. I quickly looked over towards my wife, who was sleeping soundly. I woke her, but she was very groggy, and her skin was cold to the touch. I held her in my arms until she began to respond to me. Her skin was warming back to normal. She looked up at me and asked if I was feeling okay. Then she began to cry and became inconsolable. After a while she calmed down, but she was distraught. We both got out of bed and walked downstairs.

Both of us stumbled through that day, barely speaking to each other. I stayed home from work, because I felt weak and I was worried about my wife. Later that evening, we sat down in the living room and talked about the incident.

After telling her about what I had endured, she responded by saying that she had a similar experience. She felt that the beings had removed tissue from her body and that she was very concerned. We both had examined ourselves, and neither of us noticed any marks or scars. In fact, neither of us had any pain, but we were both very exhausted.

A few days after this incident, we both received physical examinations and blood work. The results were not unusual, except my wife was slightly anemic and my testosterone level was low. In 1998 through 1999, my wife was able to conceive and deliver our son. He was born perfectly normal.

We have not experienced any further incidents. But we are both aware of what occurred and still fearful that we, and our son, may one day be abducted in the future. Thank you for taking the time to read my statement."

THIS NEXT ACCOUNT was forwarded to me in April 2018:

"This email is in regard to abductions I experienced when I lived on a farm in the Ozarks near Jasper, Arkansas.

The experience I remember vividly occurred one late night in March 1999. I was alone at the time and in the middle of sleep. I woke up and saw that there were two humanoid beings in the room. I could sense that one was a male and the other female. The male was tucking me in bed. It was a dark-skinned figure around seven foot plus in height with pointed ears. I could not make out a face. I was not afraid, but somehow felt that everything was fine. The other being, that I could sense was female, was standing at the doorway to the bedroom. Then I fell back asleep as he was tucking me in. Maybe a week or so later I noticed a scoop mark on my right hip, about an inch in circumference. The mark is still there.

I had seen activity in the sky prior to that night. On one night, there were many white lights moving quickly around in the sky. I foolishly took my flashlight and pointed it up at the sky to see if there would be a response. Well, one started coming closer to the house 28 from where I was shining the light. I was so freaked out by that and ran into the house and turned off all the lights.

In April 2001, there was a later occasion when I experienced an abduction, and this event involved sexual activity. The experience was somewhat vague, but it did include a sexual encounter with a dark-skinned female humanoid that looked very human. The female's physical features were a bit different than a normal female human, in particular the pointed ears and a strange skin texture that had a 'liquid-like' sensation to the touch. The next day, when I woke, I had intense pain and redness in my groin. It was so bad, that I needed to go to a physician, though I never told him of my experience. I was diagnosed as having severe testicular inflammation, which required a 2-day stay in a hospital. The inflammation eventually healed and has not caused me any further problems.

My wife and I have conceived three children since that event, and I have since had a fear that my children may eventually experience similar abductions in the future. I had a connection with these humanoid beings since I was young. There was missing time when I was ten to eleven years old. I remember going to bed and my bed was centered in front of a window on the second floor. I shared a room with my two younger brothers. On one occasion I closed my eyes to go to sleep. I just blinked them open and it was the next day. Maybe it was something other than lost time, but I never had anything like that happen to me since. I remember telling my mom about it after I woke up and how strange it was to me, but she did not think anything of it. But I still remember that. I have always had dreams about seeing UFOs, though I don't know how much that has to do with the abductions. I never remember going into a craft, though I know I was at a remarkable location." JK

I called the witness a few days after receiving the email. I believe that his account is truthful. I plan to go more in-depth with this experiencer in the future.

I RECEIVED the following account in April 2018:

"*In the summer of 1983, I was fourteen years of age. I lived in a rural area in central Michigan. One night for some unknown reason I woke at about 1:00 a.m. and was immediately 'drawn' to the window in my room. I looked out the window and saw a very bright light land behind my house in the edge of the woods. I figure it was about a mile out. Once the bright light landed it did illuminate enough to see a glow in the woods and adjacent field. I honestly don't know why, but I was drawn outside. If I had to guess, I would say it was an unknown 'sound' or frequency that drew me outdoors. I remember knowing I was not supposed to be out of bed, let alone outside, but I couldn't resist.*

After I walked out onto the porch and down the steps, I was greeted by a being in the backyard. It was slightly taller than me with a long neck, oversized head and large oval shaped eyes, including long fingers and toes. The overall color of the skin was greyish-green and it had no clothing. When I came upon it, it took my hand and we walked across the yard to the back fence. Once I passed the fence into the woods heading out, I do not recall anything further. But what I do remember is a feeling of friendliness and curiosity; I suppose by both of us. There was no fear. I remember the sounds of the night, and the feel of the warm damp air.

I had not thought of that night until I was in college when my friend and I went into a book store and I saw the book 'Communion' (Whitley Strieber's book) for the first time. I started hyperventilating and feeling weak in the knees as the memory flooded back. The major difference in looks is that the

"Grey" on the cover of the book looked menacing, though my experience was much different.

After that, I avoided anything regarding alien abductions, whether it in books or movies for many years. I now feel so far removed from the experience that I am comfortable relating it. I don't know what it means or if anything happened or even if it really happened. Was it possible it was a dream? I did once talk to a hypnotist when I was in my early 30's and described my memory to him. He was a member of an abduction hypnotherapy group. He indicated that based on his experience, my details were too heavy and too much physical memory for it to be just a dream. He wanted very much for me to follow up with him, but I never did.

I have done very little research, as I was checking out sites on the web, when I came across your site and decided to volunteer my information and see what came back. Perhaps this is the time for me to do further investigation on this and determine if it was real or not. I see that in the mid-1960s there were a number of sightings in Michigan. However, that was years before my time." TP

THE FOLLOWING account was forwarded to me in July 2018:

"I don't know where to begin and, honestly, I'm hesitant to even bring it up. But I believe there should be a record of my experience. I don't want any notoriety. Nothing like that. I don't want to ever speak about it again, because it scares me so much. This is the truth as best as I can recollect.

My experience occurred in the first week of June 2018, near Naples, FL. I went to sleep around 11 p.m. in a room with a friend, who was sleeping in a bed next to mine. We were sharing a hotel room. I go to sleep. Nothing unusual.

Then suddenly I woke in what seemed like a hospital room. The first thing I noticed was I was laying on what appeared to be a hospital bed. I immediately assumed I'm in a hospital. As I realize there is no way I could be in a hospital, I began to look around. I notice the walls of the room have a dark metallic color. This freaked me out because I know hospital rooms have bright colors and do not have metal walls. I was trying to understand where I was and the more things I noticed, the more disoriented and scared I became.

I then glanced to my right and I saw two people dressed in white attire. Then near my feet two more. Then to my left a person sitting in a chair beside my bed. My attention was concentrated on the person in the chair. I soon realized I was unable to move, almost like sleep paralysis. I would describe it as like being in a coma, but with complete mental awareness. I could see and hear everything around me.

The person in the chair was a human female. At least that is what she looked like. I was frightened. I remember her telling me to stay calm and it would all be over soon. She then pushes a needle into my left arm; like an IV needle but different. The needle required no tape to hold it in place, which was weird. The needle was an odd metal that gave off a strange luster. Her telling me to stay calm meant I was screwed. I was beginning to panic.

One of the 'people' standing at the bottom of the bed was holding a LED-like light on a long wire. I was told that it was used to 'decipher' who I was. The light was placed on the sole of my left foot. I didn't feel any pain, but suddenly blacked out.

I woke in the same room, not knowing how much time had passed. I was alone. Soon, someone came into the room (I never saw a door) and I began to move. I assume I walked out *of the room and was now in a hallway. On one side was a dark metal flat wall. I noticed a door. I opened it and was in a room very similar to the one I was in before. I close the door and start walking down another hallway in the opposite direction. I pass many more rooms identical to what I just came out of.*

I eventually reached an area with a giant window, maybe twenty feet tall and fifty feet wide. I approached the window and saw the clouds and surface of Earth; thinking we're orbiting the planet. I then knew I had been abducted and was in a craft of some type. I again started to panic. I looked around me and observed humanoids walking by me. But these were not human. They had olive-colored skin that appeared wet, but actually dry like that of a reptile. The faces had human features, but more ethnic. I then noticed what appeared to be 'gills' on each side of their faces. It was a startling sight; like their cheeks had been sliced open. They are quite tall, about seven feet or so and muscular. They wore no clothes or uniforms, but I couldn't tell if they were any gender.

I approached one of the beings and asked; "Is this real?" It grabbed my arm and glared at me with its golden-colored eyes. The next thing I remember was waking up on the bedroom floor in my apartment in Miami; not the hotel room near Naples! I believe I went into shock. I was suddenly sick to my stomach and shivering. I looked where the needle had been inserted into my arm and there was a small scab. I looked at the clock; it was 11:10 a.m., but I was unsure what day it was. I felt exhausted and wanted to do nothing but sleep. It turned out that I had about 36 hours of lost time. I also had a painful bruise on the sole of my left foot, where the light object touched me.

I later contacted the friend I shared the hotel room with. They said that when they woke, I was gone; but my bed had been made. All of my personal property, my wallet and phone, were gone as well. They said that they called me, but it immediately went to voice mail. There were no messages on my phone.

I have no idea what happened, but my life has changed. I have suffered extreme anxiety for no apparent reason, other than I feel that they may abduct me in the future." JJ

I contacted 'JJ' by phone. He seemed very forthright but was hesitant to discuss more personal details. He has been under a physician's care for anxiety since the incident.

IN NOVEMBER 2011, I received a telephone call from an experiencer who wanted to disclose their abduction. I asked that they compose a narrative and forward it to me. I promised absolute anonymity though I insisted that the locations and dates of the events needed to be published. In turn, I was asked not to edit any of the copy which I eventually agreed to.

When I initially talked to the experiencer I asked; "Why are you coming forward with this information?" The general reply was that they considered it an important event and that others should know that these circumstances can occur. They also wanted to make people aware of the long-term consequences that may result from an abduction. All parties agreed that the following transcript could be published:

"On Saturday, November 3rd, 2007, at approximately 8:30 p.m. my life ended. Not literally but everything I had gained and achieved to that point was taken away from me. Since that day I can only recall bits and pieces of my past but barely enough to independently get by. Fortunately for me, my mom and dad have persevered with me though, without them, I'm

not sure if I'd be able to survive on my own. I will attempt to describe what happened to me even though much of my personal history before that day has been provided by my parents and other acquaintances. The remaining information comes by way of my therapist who has extracted and recorded it from the deep recesses of my mind by means of several regressive hypnotherapy sessions. Here we go.

During the evening of that fateful day I had spent most of the afternoon attending campus events at Georgia Tech where I was in my 4th year. I was accompanied by a few friends who, like myself, were Biomedical Engineering majors. I was looking forward to continuing my graduate studies at Duke University the following year.

Around 8:00 p.m. we had just finished eating dinner at a local restaurant and decided to go to a friend's dorm room and watch TV. This is where things get 'fuzzy.' I was told (by friends and others) that we were walking on McMillan St., about a block from the friend's residence hall, when I told the group that I needed to see someone and that I would catch up with them later. The first thing I remember after that point of time is that I was laid back in a large recliner-like chair, but I had no idea where I was. My eyes were open, but I couldn't see anything other than blurry bright white light. I also felt paralyzed and could not speak. There was no sound other than a low droning that seemed to vibrate all around me. I have no idea how long I was there, but I would wake for a few minutes then dose off again. For some reason I sensed that I had been in the recliner for a very long time.

At some period, I woke to a series of 'chirping' sounds as well as the sense of something moving around me. I also noticed that I had no sense of smell though I could still breathe through my nose. Again, I would continue to dose off and on. My perception of time was nonexistent. When I would wake, I felt like I just wanted to die because I feared that I would be in this state for the remainder of my life. Anxiety and frustration overwhelmed me, but I couldn't move or yell for help.

This was all I could consciously remember about the incident. I was found forty-five hours later wandering aimlessly in one of the terminals at Hartsfield-Jackson Atlanta International Airport which is on the other side of Atlanta. I had been reported missing by my friends and my parents had already driven from our home in Raleigh, NC. The police took me to a nearby hospital where I was kept for several days. I don't remember my hospital stay. My parents drove me home to Raleigh after I was released from the hospital. This is where I have remained since.

During the past four years I have attempted to regain what I had forgotten but I am not progressing very well. I remembered my parents, my sisters and other relatives and a few flashbacks from college, but little else can be recalled. I have undergone many neurological tests and have been prescribed a few medications, but I still am unable to remember my past. In fact, I have experienced a few bouts of deep depression and afraid to venture far from home unless someone is with me. I have a tremendous hypnotherapist who has used regression therapy to help me express my feelings during my 'abduction.' Yes, that is what my hypnotherapist believes happened to me. I will attempt to describe what my regression sessions produced.

At some period during the abduction I must have been able to see my captors because I provided a fairly detailed description while under hypnosis. These 'things' were about five feet tall and had bodies similar to humans. They wore yellow and crimson overalls made of a very thin material. The heads were shaped like humans, but each had pointed chins, small noses and ears as well as a narrow mouth with dark thin lips. The eyes were larger than human eyes and circular with dark pupils, but you could tell when they focused on you because the pupils would narrow, and the eye would expand in size. I never heard them speak but they would emit an odd 'chirping.' They had bald heads and no noticeable hair. The skin was translucent with a yellow-green tint. The hands had five fingers with nails, but the thumbs were short compared to humans.

I don't remember any procedures being performed on me, but I do recall writing answers to questions on a device though I don't know how I was given the questions; if that makes any sense. Some of the questions were physics equations and others were related to human physiology. Beyond that, I couldn't recall anything more.

I truly believe we are being observed by another species. I don't know if they are alien or if they have been on this planet longer than us, but I think that we should be concerned. I have tried to avoid feeling sorry for myself, but I cannot stop thinking that I will most likely suffer permanent effects as a result of my abduction. Regardless, I can say that I still possess some hope that I will one day 'snap' out of this ordeal and move on with my life."

I had been promised exclusive access if this experiencer was able to recall further information of their ordeal. I had also asked that they keep in contact with me. To this day, there has not been significant progress.

———

THE FOLLOWING account was forwarded to me on February 3, 2021:

"In 1976 I was in the 3rd grade. That spring, my elementary school class went on a class trip to Smith Memorial Playground and Playhouse, located at North 33rd Street and Oxford Street in Philadelphia, PA. We boarded the buses and headed to the Fairmount Park section of the city. The Smith Playground has been around since the 1800s it has the world's largest wooden sliding board.

Our class arrived for the day's fun using the slide and having fun with other school kids that were there also on a class trip. Some of my classmates and I became bored, so we decided to make our own fun. We scaled a fence to another section of the playground, where we came upon a swimming pool area. In this area we can see that the pool hadn't been used in years. There were so many leaves in the pool that its color was dark green. We began throwing rocks in the pool until we again became bored, so we scaled another fence.

This next area had a pathway to our right. As we began to walk down pathway, I heard a female voice from behind me say, "stop children." When I looked back there was this "green lady" hanging from this tree. When she came out of the tree, I can see that she had scaly skin like a lizard. Her skin had a design pattern which covered her from top to bottom, as if her skin was also her clothes. She walked on 2 feet, and she had a small slit for a mouth. When she spoke to us, we can hear her in our heads. Her mouth never opened or moved.

We quickly rushed back over the fences, and I have never been back. I cannot remember all my classmates that was there. After 40+ years of questions I found one classmate that remembers this incident. There were probably 5-6 of us. Through some research I found an article from the Times Daily / Google News archive dated 10/6/1959 which describes an incident about a 'green lady' chasing school children with a knife. This does not fit the description nor the same green lady that appeared to us. I witnessed something utterly amazing and out of this world." B

THE FOLLOWING account was forwarded to me on January 30, 2021:

"I was attending our family reunion at my uncle's cabin near Land O' Lakes State Forest, Minnesota during the first week of July 1986. There were about twenty-five family members present, including my aunts, uncles, and cousins. It was the first night at the cabin and all the children were set up in tents outside. That night, my two older brothers, my cousin and I shared a four-person tent about one hundred and fifty feet away from the cabin. Since it was so long ago, I've just recently become more fearful of it.

We were all sleeping. I guess it was around 2 AM. I was sleeping on the far side of the tent and for some reason I woke up in the middle of the night. I was lying flat on my back, and I found myself looking directly into the eyes of something. It was standing on my left near my head and appeared to be studying me before I woke. The image of its face, that I can still picture vividly in my head, is like other drawings that I've seen later in my adult life. Somewhat normal-sized head, though large for its body. It couldn't have been more than four feet tall with a grey/green wrinkly face and very small nostril holes. The nose was almost flush with its face. The eyes, the frightening part about its eyes was the way that it was looking at me. Or maybe I misunderstood its reaction to my terror. It was wearing a collared uniform of sorts, similar to a trench coat that came down to the ground with seams on the front. I believe that this being was important. It was dark fuchsia/purple in color and appeared to be a dull suede texture. The moonlight made his face and coat sort of glow. The suit had a tall collar. I got the impression that this was a possible leader or overseer.

This all happened in a few seconds. I remember being terrified and immediately trying to scream but nothing happened. My brothers didn't wake. I just remember the very serious look that came over its face as if I did scream. His head tilted back like he was scorning me, or that it was somehow disappointed.

The next portion of my memory picks up shortly after. I remember being very cold, wet, and beginning to wake again. This time I am on the ground in the weeds about fifteen feet from the tent. It took all of five-seconds after waking on the ground before I remembered the face that I just saw looking down at me from inside the tent, and I let out a terrifying scream. I remember I screamed so violently that I woke my aunt who was sleeping in the cabin over one hundred and fifty feet away. I saw her silhouette after she quickly flipped on the lights to investigate. I ran to the tent and my brother was still scrambling to unzip the door. I remember the sound of the zipper when finally opening it, and he reached his arms out and pulled me in. He was asking me what was wrong. I was scared and confused. He had me lie back down. As I laid there, I told him what I had seen in the tent with us. He told me to just go back to sleep. I never told him that I also just woke up outside. That wasn't supposed to be the important part!

The next morning there were about ten other people who were talking and asking around if they knew who it was that was screaming at 3:30 in the morning. No one would say. My aunt chimed in and said she heard it too, and how she had quickly looked out the window and couldn't see who it was.

This also frightened me because I thought it was apparent to everyone!

I went and found my mom and whispered to her that it was me, and that "I screamed last night." She appeared worried and asked why. "I saw an alien." I remember the nervous pause before she whispered back "...don't say that to anyone, okay?"

I believe that there was an hour or more of lost time between the encounter in the tent and realizing that I was outside the tent and screaming. How did I end up outside the tent? How did I get wet? Was I abducted? I've never been able to answer this." K

THE FOLLOWING account was forwarded to me on February 10, 2021:

"I am a 64 year old professional woman of color who has had visitations since I was a teen. I know what happened to me and only want to discuss my events for research purposes.

The first incident listed happened at night in 1986. It is still a vivid memory of waking up on an examination table with several aliens of different heights around me under a bright light. At first I didn't feel afraid even though I knew I was not at home and believed I was on a craft. I thought I had been there several times before. They spoke to each other and myself through thought. The next thing I remember, I was still on/near the table but I felt very sad and was crying. I don't know why.

When I woke up in the morning and went to work, I felt uneasy and nervous which, is not my nature. I was casually discussing the incident with a co-worker to further calm myself down when another employee who had come in was listening to what I was saying. Suddenly, she became extremely excited and said that she was there also and saw me on the exam table. It freaked us all out and we stopped talking about it. I was a deputy-director at this agency, and I remember the name of the co-worker who also saw me.

Somehow, I believe this next incident is connected to the first one described. I lived in Queens, NY and had several visitation memories from that location as an adult. The one I will discuss happened around 1993. I woke up in the morning and there was a stillness in the room that had me feel uneasy. I had two dogs at the time and neither one was in the room with me which was strange. I stepped off the bed and everything that had happened to me the night before came back in a rush and extremely detailed.

I woke up to see very alien-like people entering my bedroom. I was not afraid at first because the first person who entered the room was my general doctor who I saw on a regular basis. The second he appeared to come in, he stepped to the side and there were several aliens who also entered. I immediately became scared and the next thing I remember was being pushed up against the wall in my room and one of them was trying to exam/look for something through my private area. My doctor seemed to be gone as I was calling out for him but the other aliens were talking calmly and telepathically to each other. They were about four or five of them in the room and by their voices, some were female. They all seemed to be some type of medical staff and wore white type clothes. The ones off to the side were about six feet, very slender and almost angelic looking with minor interest in me. The one examining me was short, very rough, wearing a hooded cloak, about four and a half foot. I kept trying to see his face, but he was trying to hide himself from me, but he appeared the most non-human looking.

I'm sure that there have been other incidents, but they all seem to blend together. As I get older, I hope that these encounters stop." - Name withheld

---

IN THE SUMMER OF 2008, I started talking to David Eckhart, a proclaimed experiencer and multiple abductee. He lived in a large home in a wooded area near Pensacola, Florida that he described as his 'dream home.' The house had a beautiful wood interior with cathedral ceilings and lots of room for his family. David was a successful carpenter and contractor who wanted nothing more than to reap the rewards of years of hard work and to enjoy life. But, for some unknown reason, he and his family were chosen to witness a world within our own.

3

DAVID ECKHART'S ODYSSEY

IN OUR FIRST conversation over the telephone, David repeated a story that he had previously told other people, including MUFON investigators. I had heard similar scenarios in the past, but there was something different about David's saga and it struck a chord with me.

Over the years, I was privy to videos, audio, screen caps and other evidence that David had collected and provided to me. His incredible story of countless abductions and home invasions by these beings has been presented on several radio interviews and featured on the television series 'Fact or Faked: The Paranormal Files.' As well, I have uploaded videos and photographs to my blog in order to gauge the reaction of the alien experiencer community. Eventually,

I was receiving a steady stream of personal accounts from other experiencers. They recognized the truth in David's story and felt comfortable contacting me.

David's ordeal began one night while he and his wife were sleeping in their bedroom. They had noticed sounds of movement around him but couldn't determine what it was. He turned the light on various times but didn't see anything. This activity continued on subsequent nights, but he could not find the source of the noise. After a week or so, he decided that his home may be haunted by spirits.

After a while David set up his camcorder, hoping that he could capture video of whatever this entity was. He knew that it would be a hit or miss endeavor, since the camcorder could only record for a few hours. After several weeks, he was rewarded. But what he witnessed on the video was more than what he could have ever thought was happening.

One weekend he decided to look at several of the videos that he had recorded. He went through dozens of hours of footage, until he noticed an anomaly quickly appear then disappear at the entrance of his bathroom. He slowed the replay to the point where the anomaly was in only a few frames. David looked closely and recognized a small humanoid entity standing in the bathroom doorway. The being looked to be about three foot in height, with a head, arms and legs; almost like the form of a child. David was astounded at what he was looking at. But he was not totally surprised, because he had encountered a humanoid entity several years before this. He was no stranger to the unexplained.

The date was May 4, 1989. David, who was born and raised in Toledo, Ohio, had recently moved to Gulf Breeze, Florida along with his best friend Ben. It is just a typical day with not much to do, so they decide to go outside and play Frisbee as a way to pass the time. Their friend, Paul, who was a college student at this time, stops over for a visit. They met Paul, a Gulf Breeze resident, only a few months before and soon became close friends.

Paul suggests they all go to Shoreline Park which is a local park in Gulf Breeze that is popular among the locals. Being a little restless and stir crazy, as many young guys are, they agree. At the park, things are casual. They talk and play Frisbee for several hours until the sun starts to set. Paul suggested that they drive to a place in the woods not far from where he and some other young people hang out. He explains to them that the sand trails are fun to drive on and there is a pond where they can build a fire and hang out. They all agree to make the trip. David decides to drive while Paul gives him directions.

When they arrived at the woods, Paul wants to drive since he is familiar with the layout of the trails. David jumps into the back seat and lets Paul take over driving. Ben is now in the front seat with Paul. They are having fun cutting donuts in the sand and just goofing off when David sees a light move across the sky at tree-top level. He thinks maybe it is a helicopter or something. It captures his full attention as it is very bright. It does not really illuminate but reflects on the tree tops and there is no sound which one would automatically expect with a helicopter or an airplane.

As he watches, the light descends down into the trees. Being a smart-ass, he jokingly blurts out; "look guys, it's a UFO!" They are looking out the windows with curiosity, but the light is now out of sight. Not giving it any more thought, they sit there for a few minutes listening to the radio. Paul then suggests; "let's go down the trail to the pond and build a fire." They all pile out of the car and follow Paul deeper into the woods when David sees a small white light off in the distance. As he watches, it flashes on and off. He tells Ben and Paul what he sees and not thinking too much about it, they all agree it is most likely someone else in the woods with a flashlight.

They finally arrive at the pond, where David and Ben stop and stare up at the sky in awe at how clear the stars are. Paul and Ben start walking around to gather wood for a fire. David then notices an orb moving through the trees. He tries to tell them what he is seeing but they don't respond to him. He quietly notices the orb getting closer, but then it disappears.

41

After several minutes they get a fire started, David and Ben walk over the pond's edge, stand there just talking. David again sees what appears to be the same orb hovering over the pond at the same tree-top level altitude. It flashes for a few seconds and then abruptly drops down as if attached to a string. Then suddenly, the orb accelerates towards David and rushes by his head while making a swooshing sound. He hollers to Ben; "look at it!" Just then, the orb speeds past Ben's face knocking him off his feet to the ground as it swoops back up to the treetops. It flashes one more time, then takes off out of sight. They were surprised, but strangely excited at the same time. They go over to Paul's side and frantically discuss what they have just experienced, though Paul doesn't seem interested. They all gather more firewood to keep the fire going when, once again, David sees the orb moving at head level through the woods and coming closer and to him. He shouts to the guys; "I'm going after it!" All he can think about is figuring out what this thing is. He barrels through the woods determined to catch it. It moves with grace and intelligence, dodging trees while picking up speed.

David finally stops running when he loses sight of the orb. But he has a strange feeling like he's being watched. He looks up and the orb appears directly above his head. It flashes as it did before, but with a bright illumination which momentarily blinds David. As his vision comes back into focus, he sees the orb cruising through the trees once again. It moves further away from him. Determined to find out what the orb is, he dashes deeper into the woods toward it. He's not feeling any fear; only an abundant curiosity.

David continues to chase the orb, when it suddenly appears to stop. He moves closer as it descends in front of him at waist level, then it moves into a small bush covered with pine straw. He could literally grab it if he wanted, but something holds him back. He's not scared but wonders if he might be hurt or electrocuted. He slowly drops down on all fours, ready to lunge at it. But then the orb darts up at his head level and flashes brightly. He begins to stand up, while regaining his vision. The orb once again takes off through the trees. David continues to chase it. It has now become like a game of cat and mouse.

As David moves closer, he vaguely sees a light in front of him. Eventually he notices a solid structure with two lights. It has a small red light that revolves slowly around the inside of it. He knows without a doubt this is not something you purchase at Radio Shack. He hears the guys in the distance trying to find his location. He tries to get their attention by yelling at them.

For a few minutes he stands observing the object, until it takes a long swoop to the left. It then dives down to the edge of the pond. He hears something drop into the water, but with no splashing sound. He scurries to find a stick, then pokes the water hoping the object will surface. As the guys finally catch up to him, David shouts, 'it's down in the water.' He climbs onto a thick branch leaning over the water. He pokes at the water, but nothing happens. In a nervous voice, Paul demands, 'let's get out of here.' Finally thinking it must be gone, David agrees to leave.

Ben and Paul had extinguished the fire making it impossible to see, but they finally make their way to a sandy trail. As they walk, David anxiously struggles to explain what the object looked like. He tells them how it flashed in his face as if someone was taking a picture. Putting his hands out, he demonstrates the size to be about the size of a softball.

As they continue walking towards the car, Ben and Paul are now about thirty feet behind David. As he continues to walk, David notices someone or something standing by a tree about twenty feet ahead of him. Whatever it is freezes and quickly moves as if trying to hide itself. David tries to figure out who or what it is. It appears to be human, but the odd eyes remind him of an owl. He moves closer. He sees that it is wearing, what appears to be, a dark jumpsuit; but it's difficult to make out in the dark. Then suddenly, he realizes that this is not a human.

When he turns and yells to the guys behind him, it takes off running. David hesitates, but soon takes off after it. He's gaining ground on the being, David notices that it runs with its fists in front of it holding what appears to be a wand or a stick. It appears to be running on its toes and not bending at the knees. As he draws closer to it, he smells the breeze break off of it. The smell of ether or antiseptic is overwhelming. He can see the back of his head as he gets closer. The being is grey with large black eyes and a slender head about chest tall. It reminds him of a child suffering from Progeria, an accelerated age disease. The feet look similar to ballerina slippers. He is so close to it but cannot bring himself to tackle it, wondering if it could hurt him. He just doesn't know what to do. Thinking he may be scaring it by chasing it, he slows down, but it keeps running until it finally runs around a bush.

By this time, the guys have caught up and Ben sees something but cannot make out what it is. David says to Ben; "run around the side of the bush and we will corner him." They both run around to the other side of the bush, but it is gone. By now, Paul is completely freaked out and only wants to find his car. He wants to get out of there as soon as possible. At that point, David believes that they experienced 'lost time.'

The next thing they remember is driving off the trail onto the main street. They were all quiet for a few minutes and then they discussed what had happened, even though none of them has ever been able to explain it. Fast forward 15 years, and David is once again confronting an unexplained encounter with an unknown humanoid or alien being.

Not long after David discovered the initial visitations, the high strangeness began to ramp up in his home. He soon realized that he and his family were chosen to be a part of an extraordinary saga. A variety of otherworldly humanoids would suddenly show up in the master bedroom by means of a portal or gateway. Abduction of the entire family occurred as often as three times a week. David was the beneficiary of a series of surgical procedures that permanently corrected a debilitating arthritic condition. He was also given the opportunity to observe underground and underwater facilities on this planet and possible Earth's moon. But it wasn't always a benign experience.

During one of David's abductions he witnessed a device that he described as a 'large egg' that had writing or graphics on it. Out of sight from his Reptilian 'guide,' he was able to quickly scribble down some of the graphics he witnessed. At one point, he states he was on a gurney or similar moving table that was in a room that contained a device that appeared to be used to transport humans; in particular, human children and smaller alien beings. The reason why or to where these beings were transported is not known but a plausible theory can be made from some of David's other encounter descriptions.

From the very beginning, it was not known to David if he and his family were in danger. During these abductions he was given the opportunity to witness his captors' routines. The reason 'why' was not told to him but, to the aliens, it seemed like it was important. A Reptilian 'tour guide' or whatever you would like to call it, was supposedly instructed to show him certain aspects of the alien habitation. In those instances when David's family was also abducted, they were kept separate from him.

David describes seeing vast underground caverns that he believed were under the Earth's surface. In these caverns, it became obvious what species was in charge; the 'Reptilian' overlords. There were other beings as well, namely a lesser class of Reptilians and various 'Greys' (not the name the aliens use). There were also other unknown species among the alien population. These caverns appeared to be mining and construction operations that used manual slave labor; including human slaves. There were also vast 'cities' in which the Reptilians lived.

David describes the small 'Greys' as three and a half to four feet tall with large egg-shaped heads, large dark bulging eyes and grey opaque skin. Many times, these beings would try to enter David's residence 'cloaked' in order to explore; though they needed to revert back to a more solid form in order to physically grasp or move objects. David explains that you could still see a ripple or mirage outline of these cloaked beings but just the general shape of the body was distinguishable. The 'Greys' appear to be a subservient, possibly engineered, race of beings; seemingly given the more menial and labor-intensive tasks. They supposedly work alongside other races, including human, in the underground caverns. They are also used as 'Earth' tour guides; taking groups of visiting alien beings on a sort of tour of Earth locations. In David's case, his house was on the 'tour'. His descriptions of how these beings would meander through his house at random times of the day and marvel at the human home and use of common amenities was fascinating and a bit comical.

At this point, the readers may feel that these are the rantings of a delusional man. But the descriptions given by an ordinary man who is placed into an extraordinary situation are tangible. I will acquiesce that some of these revelations may be on the same level to other experiencers, ex. Pamela Stonebrooke, aka the 'Intergalactic Diva,' who claimed to have had intimate relations with a Reptilian. But unlike Stonebrooke and others, David has provided more than just lip service and has never attempted to profit from his experiences.

David's 'tour guide' through the underground and underwater facilities was a certain Reptilian, who David described as a grouch who didn't like humans. David's overall impression was that he was tolerated by this Reptilian, and that it considered him not worthy of his attention. He was told that the alien presence was known by the world powers and that this 'relationship' has been going on for many years. Another interesting observation was that these entities believe in a higher being or power and that they are all connected by it. This religious connection has little to do with faith but more as a law that must be revered by all.

In 2011, the 'Fact or Faked: The Paranormal Files' television series presented an episode on David's encounters, titled 'Alien Intruder.' There was a point where the 'earthworm phenomena' manifested in the episode. David had claimed to me that after each 'intrusion' by the alien beings, his driveway would be covered with thousands of earthworms the next morning. It was so bad that David would need to hose down the earthworms onto the street and gutter (to the chagrin of the neighbors).

During the filming of the episode, David was in the bedroom and on the bed. The show crew was situated in a van outside the house and monitoring David. At one point, David exclaimed that he sensed that the alien beings were present. The equipment in the van started to go haywire; electrical interference was detected on all the monitors. After a few minutes, the interference stopped. When the crew walked out of the van, they noticed that the yard was covered in earthworms. An FBI voice analysis expert later administered a deceptive voice examination to David; which he passed on all levels.

Not long after the show aired, I invited the production's lead investigator Ben Hansen to be a guest on 'Beyond the Edge Radio.' He stated that he truly believed David and his family had experienced multiple supernatural events and that he did not think that his team debunked David's claims. He was especially overwhelmed by the earthworm incident and could not explain why it occurred.

During the last months of 2018, a new group of alien beings began to infiltrate David's life. He had moved to another house a few years previous, but there had still been some degree of visitation throughout the years. The new group consists of varying types of Greys, but for the most part there is an unknown race of beings that closely resemble humans who are part of this group. Some of these entities appear to be hybrids. They also use a different technology of portal travel. The previous group would enter David's bedroom through a gateway that manifested on the wall across from his bed.

This new group use transports that can manifest at any location. There is also specific activity that I had not previously disclosed about the older encounters, that continue to occur with this new group.

When the encounters first started, it became obvious that the alien entities were interested in David breeding with their non-human females. This became a sore point in David's marriage. There would be times when David and his wife would become intimate, then rudely interrupted; forcing David to copulate with non-human females. This eventually caused an irreconcilable situation that led to a mutual separation by the couple.

The most recent group of alien beings consists of humanoid females that closely resemble sexually mature human females. David describes them as nude well-developed teenage girls who will suddenly manifest through a transport, and then literally jump on him while he's asleep. He has managed to fight them off, as they are not very strong, and then they retreat back to the transport. David's reluctance seems to irritate the visitors, causing a bit of friction.

During the first week of February 2019, a hybrid female child was shown to David. He instinctively recognized that this child was related to him; the result of his forced copulation with non-human females when the encounters initially began. He was not allowed to touch or communicate with the child. Even though there has been no explanation as to why they are doing this, it does seem that they are holding this over his head because he refuses to allow them to breed him.

I have worked with David for almost eleven years. During that time, I have asked myself many times; "What is the reason why David has had to endure the constant contact with these alien beings?"

My best answer is that David and his family were singled out in order to be studied. Though the ordeal has lasted for almost fifteen years, none of the family has been physically injured. In fact, David was treated and cured of a serious arthritic condition. David was also privy and exposed to a variety of activity conducted by these beings.

After I started working with David, I soon became aware that these alien beings were familiar with what I was doing. For whatever reason, I was allowed to disclose much of the information provided to me. During that time period, I have been visited at least twice by what I describe as the 'Tall Greys,' even though each incident was very brief. There was no voice communication, but I was visually 'shown' several past and future scenarios.

David has described many of the scenarios he witnessed while under the control of his captors; including human experimentation and disposal. David is not the only experiencer I have interviewed and researched. One other multiple abductee described similar events that they witnessed while in the company of these alien beings.

One of my theories, that I'm sure will be controversial and ridiculed, is that many of the abductees are related to an ancient line of hybrids or evolved humans. For thousands of years, I believe that these descendants have been identified, hunted down and disposed of by various alien races. I also believe that world governments have been cooperating with this systematic genocide since the early 1950s. David's stark descriptions of abductees enduring heavily invasive experimentation (recounted as long deep incisions made in the back) and the ultimate disposal in huge, cylindrical-shaped incinerators bolsters my opinions and theory. In other words, a vast number of human abductees are never returned.

The reason why these exterminations are taking place is not an easy one to pin down, but much of what is metaphorically described in the Book of Enoch may offer some clues as to why this is occurring. The term Nephilim, the offspring of the 'sons of God' and the 'daughters of men,' may be a broader representation of extraterrestrials combining the DNA of different species. The Bible states that the Deluge was the means of destroying the Nephilim. Who is to argue that some of these Nephilim survived and continue to mix among the modern human population?

David has been constantly reminded that he should expect continued contact with these alien beings. The reason? The future and what we as a people and planet can reasonably expect. That part of the story will be left to David and other experiencers to disclose. In my opinion, the true agenda of these entities may be realized sooner than later.

THE FOLLOWING GALLERY DEPICTS A FEW OF THE AMAZING IMAGES THAT DAVID ECKHART HAS CAPTURED SINCE 2008

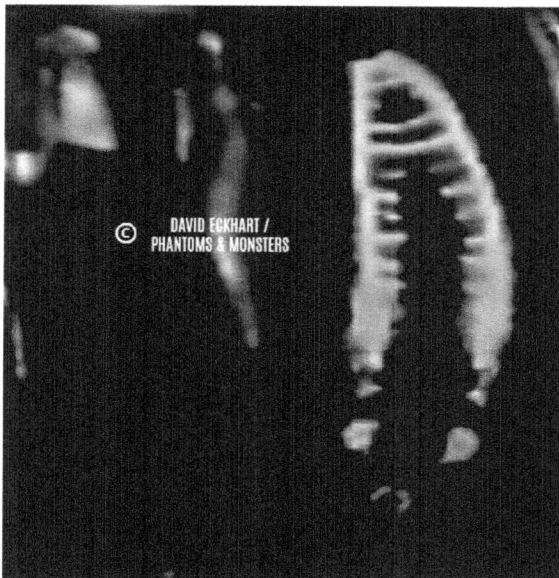

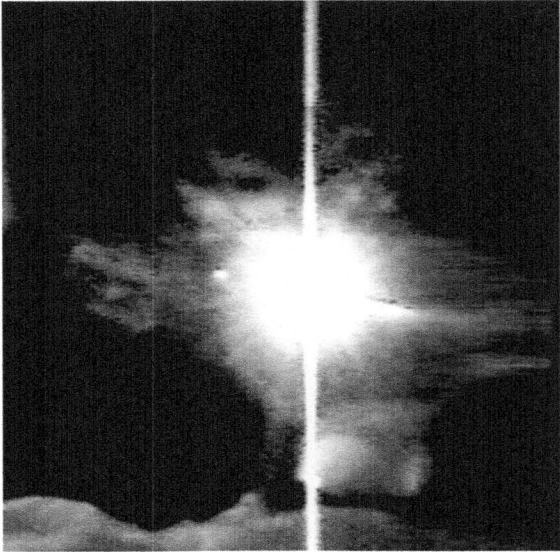
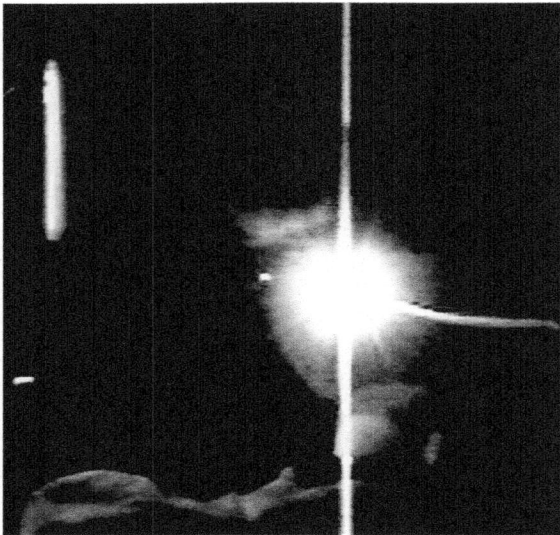

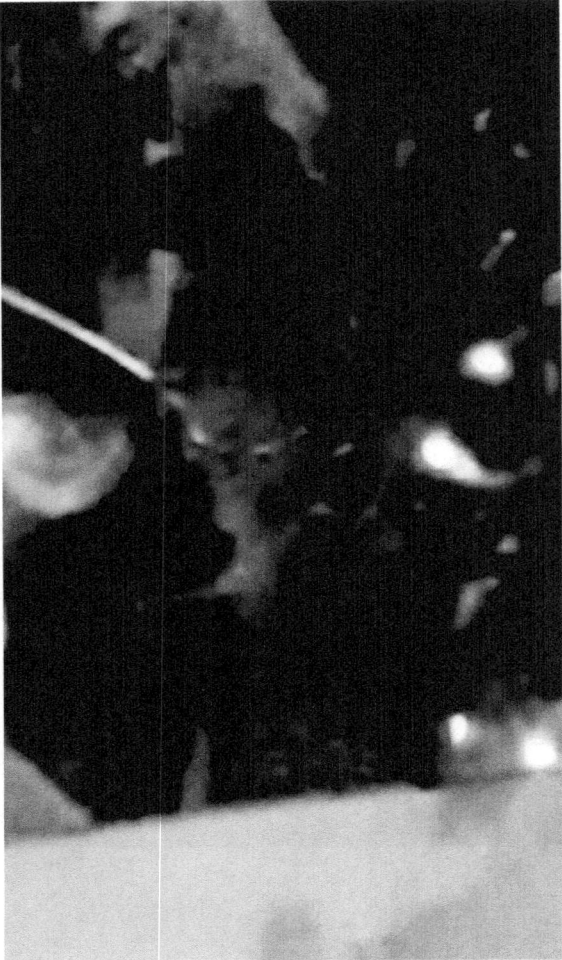

4

BEYOND THE PALE

OVER THE MANY years that I have been involved in researching and investigating Fortean events, there are a few accounts that are quite perplexing. You eventually recognize that the supernatural has no parameters; no emotional ceiling. These otherworldly incidents can result in a chain reaction that may never be resolved. Some experiencers are able to withstand the impact, but most all are negatively affected to some degree. The following accounts offer some insight as to how experiencers' lives can change.

THIS EMAIL WAS FORWARDED to me in the spring of 2011:

> "In 2005, my husband Bill and I purchased a house near Fort Campbell, Kentucky. Bill was stationed at the base and we figured that he would most likely stay since he was a wounded veteran from Operation Iraqi Freedom and had accepted a permanent position at headquarters. The house was built in

the 1890s and had a Victorian style to it though there had been several renovations and additions. We have three children, all girls, who were aged nine, eleven, and fifteen at the time we bought the house. There was a lot of space for everybody including a large yard with woodland surrounding the property.

When Bill returned from the physical rehabilitation, he didn't elaborate on how he sustained his injuries, nor did he talk about his time in Iraq. We had been married for twelve years before his deployment and I was content to the life as an Army spouse. When he returned, things had not really changed until we had settled in to the new home.

One morning I woke and noticed that Bill was not in bed. It was around 06:30 and he usually slept in until 07:15, then he would get up, eat breakfast and head to headquarters. I woke the girls for school and made my way downstairs to the kitchen to start making breakfast. When I walked into the kitchen, I noticed Bill was seated at the table, arms down his side and staring straight ahead. It actually shocked me because I had never seen him like this. I sat across the table and looked directly at him. After a minute or so, he looked into my eyes and said; "I need to tell you something."

He decided to stay home that day while I proceeded to feed my girls and get them off to school. Bill continued to sit at the table the entire time, not saying a word. I could tell that the girls were a bit confused since he did not speak to them.

When I returned home from dropping the girls off at school, Bill was sitting in the living room drinking a cup of coffee and reading the newspaper. I sat down on the sofa fearing that I was about to hear bad news. He looked at me and said; "I think I'm going to be leaving soon."

I was in shock. "What exactly are you telling me?" I asked. He looked away for a second then looked back towards me, "It has something to do with what happened in Mosul." (His division was deployed to northern Iraq near the city of Mosul). His hands and lips started to quiver. "Something happened that I can't explain. I wasn't able to report it to command because of the ramifications." He stood up and walked over to the sofa and sat down beside me. "The wounds I sustained were not from enemy ordinance. I was abducted by a group of people or something."

He explained that his platoon was on night patrol east of the city when a firefight began. Several of the soldiers went down requiring a retreat in order to get the wounded out of harm's way. At one point, Bill was alone covering several soldiers who helped others back towards the city. Things had quieted down, and Bill was about to head back towards base when suddenly he was knocked off his feet by a tremendously loud 'thud.'

The next thing he remembered he was lying face up on a table in a spacious room with bright yellow lights all around. There were four beings that looked human but were dressed in thick dark wool-like robes. Each had a small circular cap on their heads that reflected the yellow light. One of the beings told Bill that he was to become 'one of them' and that, 'he had no choice in the matter.' After that, he had no further memory with the beings.

When he became conscious, he was in a medical helicopter on his way to Baghdad. He was told he was being transported for medical treatment at another location. He was then given what he thought was a sedative. He woke sometime later in a dark room unable to move. After a time, a nurse come into the room and told him that he was in Germany and being treated for his wounds. She injected something into the IV then left and again the room went dark.

Bill thought from that time forward he was kept in a semiconscious state for a long period of time, possibly for several weeks. About a month after sustaining his injuries, he was admitted to a hospital for rehab. This was the first time that he was able to see the extent of his injuries as well as an explanation of what he was facing. Both of Bill's legs had deep long scars on the front and back.

He was told that he lost a considerable amount of nerve and muscle tissue but that he would be able to recover much of his strength and sensation through rehabilitation. He inquired about surgery records but was told no surgery was performed. He then asked how the wounds were closed. The physician said that there was no description of sutures or skin grafting in the record. The physician agreed with Bill that this seemed very irregular. For over a year, Bill tried to get answers but was stonewalled by military and medical officials. When he returned home, I was surprised Bill was able to move around as well as he did even though the scars on his legs indicated significant trauma.

As Bill sat beside me, his voice started to shake. "They will come back for me. I have no way of avoiding it." I was still awestruck by everything I had heard. I said; "Is there any way the medical staff at the fort can help you?" He looked away and said; "It's beyond that point."

We continued to live a fairly normal life despite what Bill had told me. He never mentioned the incident again and I tried to forget it. As time went by, I assumed Bill has suffered some form of battlefield stress disorder though he maintained a busy and productive schedule at home and at work.

One warm evening in July 2007, Bill left us. He had been working in the yard when all of a sudden, my youngest girl let out a horrific scream. I ran out the back door into the yard and witnessed Bill's lifeless body lying near the poplar tree. He had taken a pocket knife and drawn it across his throat. It was so *abrupt and unexpected. Bill had stated that he did not want a military funeral and wanted to be cremated. After a coroner's inquiry it was determined that Bill had taken his own life.*

Last year, I was cleaning out Bill's clothes and personal effects when I discovered an envelope in a foot locker that he kept in the garage. I pull out and read the single sheet of paper, it read; "They told me it was time to leave. I'm sorry, though I'm sure you'll understand." No. I don't understand. It's simply beyond the pale." KS

The wars in Iraq and Afghanistan have produced a large number of supernatural accounts from soldiers. The media has also reported on the many incidents of suicide among military personnel. I concur that PDST is most likely the main factor behind these self-inflicted deaths, but you have to wonder how many soldiers are being influenced by otherworldly intervention.

⸻

I RECEIVED the following account in early 2011:

"I decided to send you my description of an incident that happened to me when I was fourteen years old.

Every August my family, aunt, uncle and cousins would spend a week camping at Cabwaylingo State Forest, WV. It was a tradition because my grandparents used to do the same thing when they were raising my dad and aunt, except we were using campers. Back then we could take our bikes along and go all over the place.

In the summer of 1991, my cousins (two boys, we were all within three years of age of each other) decided to go to an area we had never been before. I remember seeing a trail sign that had 'Sleepy Hollow' on it so I suppose that was the name of the area. Most of the trail was along a small creek and it was a very thick forest. It was around noon time and it had been overcast all day. We were raised in a rural area, so our parents didn't worry too much about us exploring the park.

There was a group of large rocks near the trail, so we decided to stop and take a look. We were just jabbering when we noticed a loud humming sound coming from above us. We looked up into the trees and were hit in the face with what I describe as a blast of energy.

All I can remember is my cousins yelling at me because I had been knocked out. I asked them what had happened, and they said they were knocked out as well. We started to get scared because everything around us seemed different from before, so we headed back to the campsite.

When we got back, my mom asked me why we didn't come back for dinner. I looked at my watch, it was gone. I hadn't even noticed.

She told me it was just after 7 p.m. No wonder everything seemed strange out on the trail! We must have been knocked out for about six hours.

My cousins and I were very tired; so much so that we headed to our bunks right after eating. I was exhausted but I couldn't fall asleep. In the morning I was feeling very sluggish. My cousins slept until 11 am. Later in the day we decided to tell our parents what happened out on the trail.

To be honest, our parents thought we were playing a stunt on them by concocting this wild story about being knocked out for 6 hours by a blast of energy. I was very upset with them, especially my dad because he never let me forget about it. To this day he still thinks it was a made-up story.

My cousins and I still talk about what happened that day.

We all feel that we were possibly abducted because of some of the weird dreams each of us has had since.

In 2005, I was diagnosed with leukemia though I'm now in remission. One of my cousins was recently diagnosed with Hodgkin's Lymphoma while my other cousin has suffered kidney disease for over 10 years. We had been 100% healthy before the incident on the trail. Though we have never seen any scars or marks on our bodies we truly feel that we were physically and mentally violated by something." S

This could have been a case of overexposure to radiation, or simply coincidental. I have heard similar incidents before, where a group had an extraordinary encounter and then each developed debilitating illness later on.

THE FOLLOWING account also describes the after-effects of an otherworldly encounter.

"Dear Mr. Strickler, three years ago, my uncle (my father's brother) passed away. He lived in Lansing, Michigan at the time. I was born and lived in Lansing until I moved to West Lafayette, Indiana for college. After I graduated, I moved to Arizona (where I currently reside).

A few weeks after my uncle passed away, I received a package from the executor of my uncle's estate. The contents included several personal items that had belonged to my father and a large envelope with several photographs from the 1960s. Most of the photos were of my father and uncle at various hunting camps. The envelope also contained a letter written by my uncle to me. There was no date, but I could tell he had written it. Here is the exact content in the letter:

Please forgive me for not telling you this in person. I never knew how to explain what happened. In 1966, not long after you were born, your dad, a guide and I were in North Bay, Ontario moose hunting. We had been out in the forest for almost 6 hours and were making our way back to the cabin. It was dusk and it started to become dark quickly.

As we got nearer to the cabin, we could hear strange whirling sounds coming from the direction we were heading. I was now dark, and we could see a bright green light was shining above the cabin. We stopped walking and watched the light as it slowly circled about fifty foot above the cabin. The light was oblong in shape. I could not judge the size since there was an aura around it. The swirling sound continued also.

The next thing we remember was waking up in our cabin bunks the next morning. All of us had sharp pain around our ears and eyes. We couldn't explain what had happened to us. We packed our gear and headed for home as soon as we could.

By the time we reached Lansing, your Dad was terribly ill. Your Mom rushed him to the hospital that same night. The doctor said he had the flu, but I knew better. I didn't suffer any effects. The guide was okay also.

Your Dad was in the hospital for four days and started to feel better, but he was really never the same. I believe the incident at the cabin affected him. He would say that he continually had sharp stabbing pains all over his body. It became so bad that he could not work. Well, you know the rest of the story.

I felt that you deserved an explanation of what happened. I don't know if you should tell your Mom, that's your decision.

For as long as could remember, my father was in and out of treatment. When I received the letter, my mother had already passed away. I don't know if she ever knew what happened to my father.

My mother was the sole bread-winner for our family. We did receive some money from the state for my father's disability, but I know it wasn't much. Those payments stopped soon after my father took his own life in 1975. I wish I knew more about what happened that evening at the cabin." MM

I receive a fair amount of correspondence from experiencers' spouses and children who seek an explanation after discovering that their departed loved one had endured the effects of an encounter.

THE FOLLOWING account was forwarded to me in October 2015:

"It started a year ago on Halloween. I was out on the beach with my friends and we were having fun by the fire. Then suddenly, a flash of light. That's all anybody remembers. The events that followed, well, we have connected to that night.

It's always the quiet ones, or so I'm told. Let's call her Jessica.

Jessica was the token goth girl who was really into the paranormal and was also a realist. Days prior to the beach event, she claimed to be visited by otherworldly beings in her home at the family farm. She was a self-proclaimed witch. One of those. We believe she had something to do with all this.

After the night at the beach we all, including Jessica, woke up two towns over in the clearing of the dense woods. No car. No clothes. Just our underwear. Jessica and her boyfriend at the time, were laid near each other hand in hand. I was the first to wake up. I rubbed my hand in my hair and I felt something I damned well knew wasn't there before. I had needle marks in my arm, and it wasn't normal marks. Something happened that shouldn't have happened. Of course, I was angry and very distraught, so I began to run. It was while running I heard this muffled screech or growl. I really don't know what it was, but I had to cover my ears and close my eyes.

It was in that whatever amount of lost time, I woke up in a hospital. My family has no history of mental illness or anything of the sort. I'm a healthy person and now this happens. The nurse tells me they found me on the side of the road naked and covered in hand prints, bruises and lightning bolt-looking burn mark, that I had lost a lot of blood somehow. I was dehydrated and, for lack of a better word, taken advantage of.

It has now been about a year since that event has taken place. I've stayed off the radar. Haven't spoken to anyone about any of this, not even my family. I haven't seen or spoken to my friends since that day I woke up in the woods and now I'm losing time again and waking up every morning at 2:59 a.m. Things in my home are going missing and placed in odd places. My pets act differently now. My dog will growl for about thirty minutes every night at 5 a.m. at the window.

I have a large bay window. I feel like I'm being monitored by something and it's not human. I've never believed in any of this stuff until it happened to me. None of this made it to the news and I don't really know exactly what happened to my so-called friends either. I now reside alone and I'm trying to make sense of all of this. I don't want to completely pinpoint aliens, but I have a strong feeling whatever happened wasn't by the hands of a human. No human can make a noise like that or carry five people miles and miles away and perform those kinds of tests on them overnight." KL

This is a scary scenario, but not that uncommon. The most

interesting part of the account is that this was a multiple victim event and that none of the participants discussed what happened; not even with each other. This may have been conditioned in them during the abduction event.

I believe her life will continue with future unexplained activity. She was 'marked,' and, I'm sorry to say, this usually indicates that she will be monitored and violated throughout her life. I make these statements based on other victims I have had contact with. Some victims resign to what will happen and adjust accordingly. Others never get over the initial trauma; which subsequently may result in a tragic end.

5

NOT HUMAN BUT ODDLY FAMILIAR

MANY OF MY readers and followers are aware of the team's investigations of winged humanoids in the Chicago metro area, as well as in surrounding states. So far, there has not been a consensus of what these beings really are; alien or otherwise. To that end, I'm not going to include those recent sightings and encounters in this book.

EBEs (Extraterrestrial Biological Entities) and non-terrestrial humanoids have been an intriguing aspect of the paranormal and Ufology. Most enthusiasts tend to believe that these entities travel through interstellar space while onboard superior craft originating from another inhabited planet. That theory may very well be true. But I believe that, to a greater extent, these entities have the ability to move through time and space using star gates and wormholes; either individually or by the use of transports. This theory is based on my many years of documenting experiencer encounter and abduction accounts.

That being stated, the following accounts were forwarded to me or to an associate by experiencers and abductees.

THIS NARRATIVE WAS RECEIVED in October 2016:

"I come from a family of abductees. During my life I have had several experiences, starting with seeing a large hexagonal UFO, the kind that blends into the night sky and that you can only make out the outline as it cloaks itself. Later I experienced shining lights coming through my ceiling, and eventually I began experiencing vivid memories of piloting a ship and being of an alien race, traveling to unique worlds, some of which I called home. Over the years I have had many experiences of being educated aboard a ship (in human form), and I was always a very active, questioning and disruptive participant. I am always trying to get people on the ships to open their minds up to new ideas, think differently and also to get off the ships and onto worlds.

Most recently I experienced being on a ship once more. I was led through a corridor by a hybrid scientist, who was mostly human in appearance but with wrinkled, thick grey skin and wearing a lab coat.

We passed beside a small group of dark-skinned humanoids, canine-like people. I feel bad calling them that. They have a name, I just can't remember it. There were about twelve or so of them there. They were good looking. Not human but oddly familiar, like a very close relative of human beings with something different about them that was jarring. They reminded me of Australian aboriginal people in complexion, features such as eyebrows, eye shape, smile, lips and hair color and texture. But they had sharp canine teeth, dark dog-like noses and the men had a lot of facial hair. The men and women wore animal skin clothing. The women were mostly of older age, wore long cloaks and were hunched over and huddled together and they seemed to be feeling cold. The men wore less, more like loin cloths and were of varying ages. The scientist was very nervous in proximity to these people and tried to hurry me down the hallway. He felt they were wild animals. In a telepathic environment, you just know how others feel, they don't have to say it or explain their feelings, they just are what they are.

I was approached by one of the men very insistently, He came very close into my physical space and he flashed his eyes at me urgently; which glowed bright green like cat eyes. He was very passionate, animated and intense, and I was attracted to him, because he smelled nice. He told me (telepathically) that he was lonely, and his people wanted to get off the ship. They were genetically dying and had a very small gene pool. They needed to start meeting people. It wasn't just to reproduce of course, they were very social beings. He had a lot to say and felt that I could help explain it to the scientist because he wasn't listening.

The scientist wanted to punish the man for being disobedient and I was appalled. I had a very good feeling about them culturally as a group and felt that they would fit in very well on Earth. Both the canine man and the scientist received my feelings on the matter. In a telepathic environment it's all pretty obvious when someone hears you. The scientist was surprised at my reaction. This was another experience of dealing with Grey hybrid humans and sort of shaking my head at their oblivious ways. They know so much but there is a lot they don't understand. I was definitely more interested in the people in the corridor than whatever the hybrid scientist was taking me to do. I don't remember anything after this point. Later, I was unnerved by my attraction to a non-human. But I guess it was close enough."
Name / initials remain anonymous.

The description of a close interaction with a race other than the abductors is somewhat rare.

THE NEXT ACCOUNT occurred in Buckeye, Arizona:

"I was working on the electrical lines on one of the poles out by the substation on Old Highway 80 near Buckeye on Thursday. It was about 4:30 p.m. and I was wrapping up my work and putting my tools away, when I noticed a large object fly overhead. It cast a shadow as it passed and came down in the field across the street from where I was. The object was cigar shaped and gun metal grey and had to be at least sixty feet in length. It was almost silent apart from a whoosh sound that could be heard as it approached the ground. I was in a good position to observe it land as I was up in a bucket truck working on the high wires at the time that I noticed it. The object came to a stop and from the position I was in, it looked like the object did not come to rest on the ground itself but looked like it was floating a couple of feet from the ground.

The object was on the ground for about three minutes doing nothing when something resembling a hatch opened near the nose of the craft. After about a minute after the hatch opened, I witnessed what looked like two small children move out of the craft. Now please remember, I am about forty to fifty yards from this object, across the street and I was thirty-five feet off the ground in a bucket truck but from my vantage point I could see as these two children walked down the ramp toward the field in front of them. They were about four feet tall and skinny as hell. I mean emaciated skinny, like the pictures of the starving children in Africa that you see on the television commercials. They had big heads, they looked impossible for them to hold up with those frail bodies they had. They both wore what looked like dark blue one-piece uniforms that went down to their ankles and long sleeved down to their wrists.

The first one that came through the hatch, walked down a ramp and waited for the second one to join him on the ground. They both walked over to the fields in front of them. They seemed to be interested in the crops that were growing and it looked like they were taking samples. I slowly raised the bucket higher up in order to get a better view of what they were doing.

They apparently did not notice me (thank goodness) as they kept about their business. I observed them for about six minutes as they went about their business of walking through the field. Then a tan colored SUV came down the road and they must have seen the large object on the ground because he came to a screeching halt and threw the truck into reverse trying to see the object.

The commotion must have alerted the beings as they looked up and that is when they must have also seen me. They both immediately ran toward the craft at an ungodly speed, faster than anything I have ever seen move and they went through the hatch which immediately shut behind them leaving no trace that there had ever been a hatch right there; just smooth metal.

The object then lifted into the air, causing a cloud of dust to rise as it flew up and hovered there for about 10 seconds before flying off to the west, faster than any airplane I have ever seen fly. I stood there looking in the direction that the object flew off until the gentleman who had been driving the SUV called up to me and asked me if I had seen that thing too. I shouted out that I did as I made my way down to the truck. After getting off the truck, I spoke with the man for about ten minutes as we were both just in awe of what we saw. I have *seen many things out in the desert while I worked, but this is the very first time I have seen a UFO, much less the beings that fly them. I told my wife and she looked at me like I had lost my mind. She said I might have been mistaken and seen a helicopter landing with some soldiers getting out of it. I know what I saw and decided to write you about it." – forwarded by Manuel Navarette, UFO Clearinghouse*

NEVILLE, a 47-year-old man from Australia, witnessed a bizarre incident in a doctor's office:

"I'm from Perth, Western Australia and experienced something in or around July 2011 that may very well be similar to Raechel (referring to Helen Littrell's book "Raechels Eyes: The Strange But True Case of a Human-Alien Hybrid"). I had been having a few medical issues and was waiting at my local pathology clinic for a glucose tolerance test which takes around two hours for three separate samples.

I had arrived around 8.30 am and was fourth in line, so I began reading a magazine. My turn came and I gave my first blood sample and then given glucose concentrate to drink. The lady was surprised to see me skull the drink as most people find it rather unpleasant. Then I was told to wait in reception for an hour before they could take my next sample. During this time, I observed a young lady walk up to the front door, look inside then walk away. She did this three times during that half hour while I was there waiting for the next sample. On the forth she came in, didn't take a ticket but sat down anyway.

This young lady was around six feet tall, very pale skin to the point it was almost white, and extremely thin. I wouldn't say she was anorexic. She also wore those same sunglasses similar to what movie stars wear when trying to not be noticed. Something about her seemed rather different but I couldn't quite pick out what. As well, her arms did seem longer than usual. At least the average hands worth of extra length. I had the distinct impression she may not be entirely human so just on the off chance, I thought to myself; "You're not from here, are you?" I did this while not trying to be obvious observing her.

At that moment she whipped her head around and looked directly at me, then stood up and hurried out the door in a particularly awkward fashion. Much like a puppet on stage with its arms outstretched slightly in front. Quite a spectacle to observe and others outside looked and stared as well. At that point in time when she looked directly at me, the sun reflected from behind her, off her sunglasses then directly toward her eyes, illuminating them. Her eyes were very large! I couldn't make out the color of the iris if there was one, but those eye lids were around forty-five millimeters wide and about the same in height. I saw no reflection off the eyes themselves.

When it came time for me to provide another sample. I mentioned the situation to the woman conducting the tests (I had known her for around five years at that point) and was told; "I know who you are talking about and she needs specialized blood treatment. But keep it to yourself." My father used to work for the same company doing biological transport as a courier. She knows my father. I've just had cause to go for another blood sample 7th January 2016 and will be having another GTT test this week. I hope to see that same young lady again.

All details I have provided here are true and accurate descriptions of events experienced at the time on that day. I thought that may be of interest to you."

I believe many of us have observed someone who just doesn't fit in the scheme of things. It's interesting to read or hear how observers react to these encounters.

I RECEIVED the next account in May 2018:

"I have been wanting to tell someone who cares about what I seen for a very long time. Someone that will be open-minded and not judge. It was many years ago, but I remember it as if it was yesterday. I was at work in Greensboro, NC, when lunch time rolled around, and I left for my friend's house in Allen Jay (High Point).

Anyway, it was the early spring, a beautiful day at approximately 12:15 p.m. I believe it was 1992. I drove on Nance Ave on the way to my friend's house. Everything was fine and I was very close. All of a sudden there was an 8-9 foot being (maybe even taller) standing on the left side of my car on the side of the road. I couldn't believe my eyes. I slowed down to look up at it. The eyes were kind of large and shaped like the normal cat's eyes. It was so black and dark. I wore cloak and had on a toboggan type cap. It was so black that it kind of melted in together with the cloak. No hands were visible or feet. It was just standing there looking straight ahead at something. As I drove by slowly, I kept watching in my mirror at what I was seeing. Then it quickly turned and was looking at me.

Now the road I was on is somewhat hilly with small hills. I was so fascinated with what I was seeing I wanted to go back. I never took my eyes off of the being as I could see just a little bit of him. As I went to turn around, I still had a visual on it. As I whipped my car around, maybe 3-4 seconds with *my eyes not on the being, it completely disappeared. I was scared, but also fascinated.*

I think the only person who believed me was my friend. She said when I came flying through her door my face was very white, and she knew something was wrong. I tried to calm down before I went back to work. I have never seen anything similar since." DB

Most experiencers become quickly frustrated by other people not taking them serious about their encounter. One can only imagine the number of individuals who decide to stay quiet in order to avoid ridicule.

HERE IS an eyewitness statement of a shapeshifting being in the Point Pleasant, WV area; just one month before the Silver Bridge collapse. I received this account in December 2016:

"One chilly day in November of 1967, my parents decided to go to a private event in Point Pleasant, WV. We were southbound on the highway by the Ohio River on the W.Va. side. It was a long ride and my butt was starting to go numb, so I was shifting my position. I then caught sight of something from the corner of my eye. On the side of the road, in a thin stretch of woods between the highway and the river was this bum; or I thought he was a bum. He was wearing a brown flannel shirt and grubby, baggy brown pants and a brown hunting hat with ear flaps down. He was running alongside our car! I checked the speedometer. We were moving at 35 mph! I kept looking at him and he kept running alongside the car. Then suddenly he turned and looked at me. It looked like he was wearing welding glasses or old-style motorcycle

goggles. They were brown-framed circles with bright red lenses.

He kept up with us for several hundred yards until a wide bend in the road moved us apart and I lost sight of him. About two-seconds later my brothers started yelling; "The man! He's flying! Look! That guy is flying!" It wasn't the same guy. This one was in a silver suit with wings. He held his arms up by his chest. I don't know how he was controlling his flight. He shot straight up out of the woods, then leveled out and headed towards the east. He had red eyes, but not like the running man. The flying guy's eyes were glowing very brightly. He flew behind a hill and that's all we saw of him." BB

I was later able to talk to the eyewitness. He now believes that this was what people were referring to as 'the Mothman.' But was it the running man shapeshifting into this winged humanoid? Was it an alien being?

THE FOLLOWING WAS FORWARDED to me by an associate:

"This story begins on a cool summer night in the city of Issaquah, WA in the year of 1989. I was a police patrol Sgt. on night shift with a squad of four officers. The night had been uneventful until approximately 3:00 a.m. Another officer, who I will identify as John, and I responded to an alarm at a business located in an exclusive shopping area known as Gilman Village. It is made up of older homes and buildings that were moved into an area near Issaquah Creek connected by a wooden walkway. Gilman Village is a very popular shopping destination for tourist and locals alike. I enjoyed

walking through the complex while working night shift for the exercise and to window shop at the many interesting stores.

Receiving alarms at the different businesses throughout Gilman was common and most of the time uneventful but on this particular night there was nothing common or uneventful about it.

John and I responded to the alarm at a business which was then called the Levi Coat Factory. We performed an outer perimeter check of the building and found it to be secure. Dispatch made phone contact with the owner who declined to respond to allow us to check the interior of the building. John and I returned to the parking lot located on the northwest side of the complex. This is the area where we had parked our patrol units. John and I stood outside and carried on a conversation in the dimly lit parking lot approximately sixty to seventy feet away from the buildings in that portion of the village. The buildings were to my left and to John's right.

Both of us noticed an unusual movement near the eves of one of the buildings. It was a ball of light about the size of a cantaloupe moving slowly from left to right following the area just below the eves. The light was very intense. We stared at the light until it disappeared around the south side of the building. Goosebumps prevailed. Officer John and I looked at each other with eyes wide open, each asking at the same time; "Did you see that?"

What we had seen was strange enough, but nothing compared to what we were about to witness. While we stood and talked about the strange event, our eyes were once again drawn to the northwest corner of the same building only this time it was the lower corner. A perfect ball of very intense light approximately one foot off the ground floated around the corner. The ball was about four feet in diameter and once again a perfect sphere. The thing that made me speechless was what I had seen inside the sphere. Walking upright was, for the lack of any other word, a creature walking. The arms swung back and forth, and the hands were turned with its fingers pointed to the rear. As the sphere progressed along the side of the building it went behind bushes that grew in between the sphere and the parking lot. The light was visible through the openings of the bush and it was very clear that it was not being projected.

As I recall, at least a full three minutes passed before either John or I could speak. To put it lightly we were terrorized by the unknown. This event changed the way I think and look at stories by others claiming encounters with the unknown. John and I never spoke about the event until 2010." RJC

I always welcome encounter reports from police officers. It immediately adds credibility to the account, especially when they are astonished about what they had witnessed. The associate who forwarded the account was able to talk to the witness, which is another plus to its veracity.

THE FOLLOWING account was forwarded to me in March 2017, after Stan Gordon was our guest on 'Arcane Radio':

"I had an 'incident' happen about eight years ago when I was living in Shasta County, CA. I figured you'd be interested in reading it. One evening while I was watching television in my living room, I noticed a bright red flash come through the window nearest me. The flash came from my backyard. I looked outside and was shocked to see what appeared to be a flat circular object hovering, then landing, in the field behind my garage. There were blue and white lights flashing *intermittently around the object. There was mist or smoke rising from it. I first thought it might be a large helicopter, but it was silent. After a few seconds, the object instantly vanished in another bright flash.*

It stunned me and left me wondering what I had just witnessed. I waited for a few minutes, then went outside with a spotlight to take a look. I am single, so I was alone. There are a few houses on the other side of the field, but the distance to the nearest property is about a quarter mile. I didn't see any other people investigating the lights. There was nothing to indicate that the object had landed in the field, so I decided to wait and look some more the next day.

I didn't find any evidence the next morning. I estimated that the object had been about 50 or so feet in diameter. That night something happened that has changed my belief in the unknown.

I was sitting in the living room watching television at about 9:30 PM, and once again I was stunned by another bright red flash coming from the backyard. I immediately got up from my chair and looked out the window. There was a full moonlight, so I noticed that in the same location that I saw the object land the night before, there was also something moving around. I didn't know what to think or what to do. I wondered if I should call the authorities, but then I'd have to tell them about the flash of light and what I had witnessed the previous night.

I just sat there with the lights and television off for several minutes. I then started to hear dogs barking in the distance. Then suddenly I heard something hit the side of the garage, and then a deep groaning sound. I sat there quietly, when I saw a faint shadow move across the window. The window is almost 7ft from the ground, but the shadow completely blacked out any light. It was moving towards the front of the house. I got up and looked out the dining room window. There was a huge hairy creature illuminated by the light on the utility pole. It must have been eight to nine foot in height and a massive body. This had to be a Bigfoot! As I continued to watch this creature, it walked away from my property, then into the adjacent field. I went upstairs and sat at my bedroom window, just waiting to see if the creature returned.

The next morning, I walked around my property looking for tracks. I did find an indentation in the ground that measured fifteen inches long and six inches across, but I'm not sure if it had been from the creature. I didn't find anything unusual, other than a cinder block laying by the garage. It had to have been brought there.

To this day, I have only told a few friends about the incident. I wonder if the Bigfoot had come from a UFO or that it came on its own." CK

Pennsylvania UFO and Bigfoot investigator Stan Gordon has documented several Bigfoot sightings prior to and after UFO activity. I have also received a few similar incident reports. Is Bigfoot an EBE? The evidence seems to suggest a strong possibility that some large hairy humanoids are connected to UFOs, but are these actually Bigfoot?

———

MY SON and I were going through a few boxes of documents that we had placed into storage during our move in spring 2016. I found a bunch of printouts I had made of emails that were sent to me not long before I started the blog in 2005. Most were fairly mundane, but one was quite interesting. In fact, I remembered when I first read it, but didn't know what to make of it. I don't recall if I every contacted the witness. But anyway, I'm offering it to you:

"Before I begin, I would like to say I am actually a skeptic and try to rationalize what I feel is not rational. That being said, most, if not all of my first-hand odd experiences occurred before I was an adult. I am now 31 and what I remember of this incident is still quite vivid. I am simply looking for the truth, so I hope you understand that what I am about to share is one hundred percent factual, not embellished in the slightest. I hope you or someone else can shed some light on what I actually saw here.

Back in 1990 I was a 16-year-old high school kid and athlete, with a normal middle-class family living in a suburban neighborhood in Bucks County, PA. I remember it being in Autumn because there were leaves all over the ground and the crisp air is still fresh in my memory. I had just finished hanging out at a friend's house just down the road from mine. It was about 7 p.m. or so as it was dusk, about the time the street lights starting to come on. The neighborhood I lived in was a medium-sized development built just after WWII. Everyone knew everyone, and traffic was light due to the road ending at the edge of the woods.

As I was walking home, I noticed something dash out of the bushes on the left side of the road. It moved rather quickly, but in a strange manner. My first instinct was that it was an injured dog, possibly hit by a car and dragging its hind legs. Even though it was still far ahead of me, it startled me, and I stopped dead in my tracks. As I did so, it stopped in the middle of the road. I then got a very good look at it. It was a baby. I remember thinking; "How the f**k did this baby manage to crawl out of a house and in to the middle of the road?"

I started to quickly make my way towards it in order to get

it off the street. I remember being panicked, but somewhat amused and bewildered as I trotted towards it. As I got nearer, I started to realize that what I was running towards, and what I was looking at, was not a normal 'baby.' At least that was what I thought just before I suddenly froze. The 'baby' snapped its head around and, with its weird empty eyes, stared at me with a maniacal grin. I just looked at it, waiting for its next move. At the same time, I was thinking I'd better haul off in the opposite direction. I backed off several feet but continued to watch this aberration. It was about the size of a one-year-old child, but naked and totally hairless. It had muscular arms and weird short legs that dragged behind it. It also looked wet and shiny, like a glaze or thick oil was put on it.

After several seconds, it quickly scurried away with its stumpy legs dragging back and forth behind it. It crossed the street, then through the yard of a house, but quickly disappeared. I figured it made its way into the woods behind the house. I stood there motionless and shocked. In fact, I leaned against a mailbox post until I regained my composure. When I did, I felt like I needed to get home as soon as possible and sprinted in that direction. When I got home, I went directly into my room. I didn't even eat dinner and told my mom that I wasn't feeling well. I was in a strange mood for several weeks after that. Anyway, the story doesn't end there.

A few years later, I was told that the woman who had lived in the house where the deformed baby dragged itself into, was thought to have dementia. She would often call the police and accuse the neighbor kids of breaking in to her home and hiding in the basement. The police would investigate, but never found any evidence. I don't know what eventually happened to her, but I wonder if the 'baby' may have been antagonizing her and living in her basement? Have you ever seen or heard about anything like this?" HT

I remember wondering if, at the time I received this email, this was a spiritual being or a flesh and blood humanoid. Some people may suggest that this was a demon or a malevolent entity, with no indications of being an EBE. This 'baby' may have been a mutation, or a human hampered by a birth defect; but that still leaves the question as to why it was roaming the neighborhood.

———

A COLLEAGUE in New York forwarded the next report:

"I'm from east Long Island, NY and single. On a recent Summer night, I was lying in bed unable to sleep when a very bright white light entered the room. Then several humanoids appeared in my bedroom and stood by my bed. These beings were about four-foot tall, wide in the torso, with large heads, large black eyes, no ears, or hair with dark bluish-grey skin. Their hands were very wide with thick fingers and nails. They wore white robes down to the floor. They asked me to come with them and I followed them down to the street.

There I saw a group of women, maybe two dozen or so, slowly walking down the street. All appeared to be in a trance and were walking in the direction of the beach. I also felt drawn to the water.

When I got there, I observed four brightly lit disc-shaped objects hovering over the surface. A tall beautiful female with pale skin and wearing a long flowing black hooded robe appeared in front of me. I was called by this being and asked to conduct a 'test.' I soon found myself standing by the foot of my bed with the stocky beings attempting to stick me with a long needle. It was inserted into my upper chest and an opaque yellow liquid was extruded from me. I remember waking midmorning with a terrible headache.

I have no idea why this occurred. I couldn't find any marks, but I do experience intense dizzy spells and have problems eating some days." JN

This report of being among multiple abductees is disconcerting, let alone when they are in a trance and walking down the street. I suppose that this could have been a dream or vision. But can adverse physical effects continue after an intense dream?

THE 'GRINNING MAN' phenomenon has been prevalent in Ufology lore since the reports of strange incidents in the Point Pleasant, WV area in the mid to late 1960s. I received this next account in July 2017:

"In early April of 2017, I required a CAT scan at a local hospital here in Nashville, TN. I'm sitting in the waiting area with a couple of other people. Each person was called and taken in by a woman. I was the last one left, waiting for an unreasonably long time, so I kept looking for anyone to call me for my scan. After a while, I became restless, so I got up and looked in the CAT scan hallway, but nobody seemed to be there. I walked over to another area with a reception desk, but no one was there either. I thought they must all be on a lunch break and I was not happy. So, I went back to my seat.

A few minutes later, The CAT scan hallway door opens and I'm expecting to see that same woman asking me to come in, but this time a man came out. The only words that I can write to describe him are that he was bizarre and downright hideous looking. Exceptionally tall and thin, he had on a strange looking suit and tie. His eyes were just slits, his skin was scared, and he was completely bald. My initial thought was 'there is no way that this guy works here.' He looked so horrid. He would simply scare children and half the people that needed scans. He also had the most insidious wide grin. I really wasn't scared, but completely perplexed why this guy would be allowed to work in this environment.

He called out my first name and took great pains in pronouncing it. I followed him and then sat on the scan table. He went around the corner but kept looking at me through the window. Then he was gone. I waited for several more minutes, until two other men came in to do my scan. I don't know why, but I didn't ask about the weird-looking man. In fact, I actually forgot about him. That was until I was at a friend's home a few weeks later and her sister dropped in for a visit. She mentioned that she worked at the same hospital in the Radiology Department. I asked her who the bizarre man that works there was. She gave me a bewildered look and told me that she had no idea what I was talking about. She asked me to detail his appearance to her. She again confirmed that no one with that description worked there and became somewhat hostile at my insistence at what I saw.

A week later, I went to my doctor for the results. His words were "I'm sorry, this is quite unusual. Your CAT scan is missing. The scan and report vanished and couldn't be found.' Now I wonder if the weird grinning man was responsible." NL

I RECEIVED the following account in June 2013. An interesting aspect of this incident is that it occurred in Hebbronville, Texas; a town where a lot of strange activity has been reported. I have received accounts of small T-Rex-like cryptids and other strange beings from Hebbronville eyewitnesses over the years:

> "This all happened last week on the 6th and 7th of June, 2013 around 11-12:00 at night, both nights, in Hebbronville, Texas. Thursday evening, I went to a friend's house to do a couple loads of laundry. She only lives a few houses down, so I waited until the kids were asleep to go. My oldest was still awake and I asked him to keep watch as the 'man of the house.' I had to do the same as a kid with my siblings quite often. I figure he's ten so he's old enough. My husband was at work doing the night shift. I left around 10:45 p.m.
>
> As I was leaving, I felt scared to leave them. I felt something wasn't right. But I thought I wasn't going to be far and would come back to check on them. So, I put the clothes in the washer and went back home immediately. My oldest son was in the living room playing with our cat. Everything seemed fine and I figured I was being silly. So, I went back to my friend's house and I stayed until around midnight. When I got home, everything seemed fine. My son was asleep on the couch, so I went to bed and that was that.
>
> The next day my son tells me he saw something the night before while I was out. He said he was playing with the cat when he noticed something peeking into our living room window. He said it was an alien. Tall and skinny with dark grayish-green skin. It had a funny shaped head. When it left our window, he said he crawled over and peeked out. He said that he saw other beings walking around and peeking into people's windows. One stood watch while the other did this. My son said he was scared but didn't give me any more details. I was upset that he didn't call me at the time. So that evening I stayed up all night to keep watch. I would go outside and check the area. I checked on the kids all night. I

was exhausted by 4:30 a.m. Nothing out of the ordinary happened.

The next day, which was Saturday, I came over to my friend's house again. The kids and hubby went out of town. So, I bring up the story my son told me, and my friend tells me she had an encounter the night before. I got all excited. She tells me it happened after midnight. She was sleeping on her couch in the living room. It's a small 2-bedroom house. From the couch you can see the back door. She was having trouble getting to sleep. During this time, she says she heard the handle to the back door turn like someone was trying to get in. They turned the knob and she could hear them push the door. Then she noticed the lock moving. It was opening! She got scared and remembers blacking out right when she was feeling panicked. Later she remembers 3 beings in the house. She described them exactly as my son did. When I told her my son's story, I didn't really give details about their appearance. But she was able to describe the same thing. This confirmed my son wasn't lying. My friend and son had no contact at all during their experiences. She described them as slimy looking with dark greenish skin. They were tall and thin. She said she just laid on the couch in a groggy state as they walked around her house. Those were bits and pieces she remembered the next day.

Sunday I was talking to my son about what he had seen, and I told him my friend's story. He made a face and said he made the whole thing up. Now I would believe that if my friend hadn't told me her story. The fact that they both described the same thing tells me it truly happened. I am confused now but know my friend wouldn't lie. She isn't into aliens and UFOs or anything like that. So, she has no need to make anything up. I find both stories fascinating. I hope you can make sense of it." M

Is this another strange event that can be added to the annals of Hebbronville, Texas? Is it possible that this was some type of thought projection through the son? I leave it up to the readers to decide.

I RECEIVED a telephone call from an eyewitness in Tennessee on 2/26/2018. The account he gave me was one of the strangest I have ever heard or read:

In early summer 1985, the witness 'RO' and two other friends were in the Land Between the Lakes National Recreation Area. They were exiting the park while traveling south on Rt. 49 (Woodlands Trace Byway) towards Dover, Tennessee. The three men were sitting together in a Ford Ranger. The driver 'JM' and 'RO' sitting beside each other. The other friend 'TG' was sitting on the passenger side. It was early evening and still light.

As they approached a curve in the road, an older model gray- colored sedan was in the opposite lane coming towards them. The sedan slowed as if the driver wanted to talk. As JM and RO looked at the other driver, they were soon horrified at the sight.

RO stated that the other driver had wild bushy hair and wore glasses. When the 'person' turned their head towards them, the eyes appeared to be oversized. The driver's window was open. Suddenly this being or humanoid extended its head out the window as the neck stretched to an incredible length. The face shapeshifted; taking on a bizarre contorted appearance. The head was now upside down and looking at them, at the same time making loud 'woo-woo-woo' and howling sounds. It was a dreadful vision.

RO and JM were totally shocked and in utter fear, to the point of tears. JM accelerated away from the other vehicle. At the same time, the other friend TG never reacted to the sight of this being. He was either asleep or was immobilized somehow. He had no idea of what had just taken place.

The encounter was so disturbing to RO, that he literally begged JM to turn around and go back so that RO could kill the being with his rifle. RO told me that he was never felt so repulsed before; that he had an overwhelming reaction and that he must eliminate this abomination. JM refused to do so and continued driving away towards town.

RO stated that the incident remains fresh in his mind and that he will always be fearful that he may once again encounter the being. He asked me to contact JM in order to verify the event, in which he did; though he refused to elaborate on the encounter.

NOTE: The Land Between the Lakes National Recreation Area, which resides in Kentucky and Tennessee, is well-known for bizarre activity; including upright canines and Bigfoot.

I FOUND the following account while digging through my old UFO files. I know it was sent to me, but I have no idea where it came from:

"I was asleep one night in November 2006, in my two-bedroom two-story detached house on CFB Cold Lake, Alberta, Canada. At about 1:00 AM I was awakened by two human-looking beings coming from the direction of the window and approaching my bed. One was tall and slender dressed casually, very neat and clean with an aura that *illuminated the room. He had short fair colored hair and light-colored clothing. He had a Nordic appearance. The light seemed to emanate from behind him and enabled me to see pictures on the wall in a room. The room was normally pitch black at night with the blind pulled down. On this being's right was a shorter less visible being who didn't have an aura and appeared unkempt, not sure because he was less visible. They were talking to each other as they approached my bed. Then the taller being turned from the shorter being and spoke to me in calm voice and said; "Where are the stairs?"*

I was still groggy and confused. I gestured toward the bedroom door to my left with my left hand in response to his question. They turned toward the door and walked through the closed door which appeared open or see-through in the aura light which made even the hallway and stairs visible to me. They continued talking to each other and walked down the stairs and as they walked their footsteps and voices faded and the light faded until there was complete darkness and silence. I was left wondering what just happened and if I had left my downstairs house entrance unlocked. I thought to myself; "Of course I didn't leave it unlocked," and I thought; "I'm not going downstairs to follow them." I was little fearful as I don't know what these beings were.

During the encounter I didn't feel scared. It was only in retrospect I started thinking about what just had happened I became a little spooked, but not enough to stop me from sleeping. They seemed nice, not angry or mean.

I had a similar encounter about a year after when a similar being came through the closed bedroom window. Again, I think he wanted to know where the stairs were. As they came through the window, they moved the blind aside and popped their head in and looked at me, like he recognized me, then smiled and came in. He approached the bed. There was only one this time.

The beings weren't from another era or time period or didn't appear to be." Anonymous

I doubt that these were spiritual beings, though I cannot discount it. I have heard and read other accounts of Nordic beings acting nonchalant with witnesses. My best guess is that there may have been an intersection of realities somehow. It's an interesting and quirky encounter.

———

I RECEIVED this short inquiry in May 2018. It's a bit disturbing as well:

"I have been visited by various alien entities since 1974. I had missing time on several occasions over the past forty-four years and have been abducted countless times.

I did have one experience in 1999 that gives me reoccurring dreams; during a night at my home in northern Wisconsin. I remember being taken from my bed, being led into my living room. I remember seeing things around me. I was shown a young girl twelve years old or so. I remember knowing that I was the child's father. I remember being so angry, realizing that I was used over the years to create this abomination. I had, for as long as I can remember, kept a gun under my pillow. I had it in my hand. I was so angry that I was able to pull free and I shot the girl. I am a law enforcement officer. Since that day, I put it away, and I have trouble handling it.

After shooting the girl, I remember being punished. I have had painful lumps in my arms that constantly hurt and

remain to this day. All this time I have hesitated to tell anyone else about any of my encounters. I did report my story to MUFON. They called me and made me feel like a criminal."
Name withheld

I was able to speak to this experiencer who proved to me that he was a police officer. I would like to believe that I wouldn't have responded in the same manner as he did, but he is deeply frustrated by the continuous encounters. I was able to talk to this man since the initial telephone call. He is receiving medical treatment; emotionally and physically.

I WAS RECEIVED this next report in July 2018:

"Back in the Spring of 2016, a few of my friends were talking about their experience with some weird creature, in the desert southeast of Tucson near Vail, Arizona. The descriptions sounded a lot like Mothman, though this creature had no wings. I was skeptical, but I didn't want to doubt my friends because whatever this was had really scared them. They said that they believed it was some kind of alien being.

Later that year, during the Winter, these sightings were far from my mind. I was visiting a friend who lived in Vail. I stayed over late that evening. At about 2:00 a.m., I left their house to drive about twenty-five minutes down I-10 towards home. Driving about fifty miles per hour, while approaching a rise in the road, I saw a silhouette. Before I even processed that I was observing something I soon realized that I had slowed and eventually stopped on the shoulder to get a better view.

It was about twenty yards or so away, standing almost in the middle of the road. Because of the rise in the road I could only see this form from the hips up. It was very tall and looked human-like. Very skinny, with long thin arms and skin that was dark, leathery and dry; though there was a 'sheen' to the body. The eyes were a reflective red color. I couldn't tell if it was looking at me or not. There wasn't another car in sight at the time.

I'm usually very calm during emergency situations. I'm interested in unexplained phenomena, but confronting this thing, the panic switch flipped. My mind is telling me to hit the gas, but I just sit there, staring at this thing. I looked down for a second, considering turning around and driving back to my friend's house. I put the car in first gear, looked back up and the being was gone. I immediately drove towards my house. I was shivering uncontrollably the whole way home. I pulled into the driveway, walked in the kitchen door, and became violently ill. I literally passed out in my bathroom.

I didn't wake until about 1:00 pm that day. I dragged myself off the bathroom floor and immediately went to bed. I was totally exhausted and just wanted to sleep. I rarely left the bedroom for the next five days. I had no appetite and it seemed like every bone in my body ached. One of my friends eventually came over and helped me into the living room. I ate a little bit, but I was still very tired and despondent. I didn't tell her or anyone else what I had encountered. I just said that I had the flu.

Do you have any idea of what I observed out in the desert? Have you heard of similar creatures?" ML

I contacted 'ML' by email and later by telephone. She seems reluctant to discuss this event and is somewhat fearful that this being may seek her out. The being didn't seem to be an apparition, and her description suggests that it was an actual corporeal entity. It is interesting as to the high number of bizarre cryptids and humanoids that are encountered in the desert.

THE FOLLOWING account was sent to me several years ago. I never got in contact with the eyewitness, since they lived in the UK. It may be possible that it was a third-person account, but I can't proof it. Anyway, it was just one of those encounter reports that was sitting in my incoming report file. I just wish I had more background on it:

"I am hoping that there are other people who may have experienced the same thing. It involves my brother and this account is pieced together after I became involved. I have discussed it with other people who remember it, mainly family members. I have not sugar-coated it or added anything, this is exactly as we remember it.

I grew up in a former coal mining town in the north of England. To give a little more background, this town is located between the cities of Newcastle-Upon-Tyne and Durham. This area has had its share of UFO activity. This story goes back to when I was nine-years-old in 1997. At that time, I used to help my mother babysit my newborn cousin who lived in the same street. On this particular occasion, a Saturday night, my brother had decided to come too. He was eight-years-old at the time.

It was a normal evening, nothing out of the ordinary. My mother put the baby to bed around 8:00 pm and we started watching a movie. My father called to tell me that my mother had forgotten something in the house and asked me to go to pick it up. I left and then decided to stay with my father for an hour before going back. Then, the phone rang. I answered it as

I was closest, and it was my mother who was concerned about my brother who was freaking out.

I passed the phone to my dad and he said we would come get him. As we arrived, we found my brother on the couch, all white and crying with fear. My dad asked him what had happened, but he could only speak gibberish. However, he was able to say; "I never want to stay in this house again. I want to go home." My brother and I shared a room, and I still remember him crying all night. Needless to say, it was a sleepless night for the whole family. My brother never talked about what happened and true to his word, he never slept at my aunt's house again.

Several years later, when my brother was about sixteen, he decided to open up about what had happened that night. We were alone in the house while my parents were on holiday. I asked him, just as I remember it, and he paused the computer game he was playing, stared at the pause screen and said, "Mom sent me to check on our cousin (the baby), so I went upstairs. I didn't turn the light on as the living room light was enough and I went into the baby's room. Everything seemed normal at first. Then, I felt it. A strange presence, as if something was behind me. It wasn't a feeling that something was there, but rather, an unknown certainty. A heavy breathing sound started and at first, I thought it was the baby snoring, but it was too heavy; sort of like Darth Vader but more aggressive. I turned to the door slowly and saw a figure. It was dark but I could tell that its skin was green on its right side. What scared me most were its glaring red eyes that just stared at me. I hid behind the door thinking that I was going to die. It just stood there, staring at me through the crack in the door, its head turning to keep track of me with its red eyes. Those red eyes just staring at me. It seemed to stay there for about twenty minutes, and I didn't move as I thought it would hurt me.

Then, it just disappeared. I think it may have opened the window and jumped out. I only realized it had gone when the heavy breathing stopped, and the feeling of terror disappeared."

Although my brother had claimed it felt like the incident lasted twenty minutes, he had literally been gone for one or two minutes.

I have to admit his story was unsettling and I imagine that people would think it's all made up. It's quite a lot for a nine-year-old to remember. But he claims as he got older, he was able to describe it better, as this night has always been on his mind. My aunt was never told this story, but one day I asked her if she had ever seen or heard anything strange in her house, to which she replied; "Once when your brother was a toddler, he fell down the stairs. When we asked him if he was OK, he replied that the man with the red eyes had done it." Although he was very young, he remembers it clearly to this day. He recalls looking back up the stairs, to see a figure standing there, just staring at him with those glowing red eyes. So, it seems it wasn't the first time he had encountered this being.

My brother also claims to have had dreams about this ever since the babysitting incident occurred. One dream in particular was that he was playing with our Labrador in my mother's home office in the evening. Then, out of the corner of his eye he noticed a figure walk past the door in the dark. The dog went crazy, snarling and barking; with all of his hairs standing on end, like a dog does it when it tries to make itself look bigger when under threat. But looking out into the darkness to see what the dog was barking at, there they were. Those staring red eyes.

For years, we have tried to make sense of it, doing a lot of internet research, writing on forums and so on, but never came to any conclusions to what it was. I understand it is a lot to read, but maybe someone, after all these years, can shed some light on the whole thing?" SB

I believe I forwarded the account to another researcher in the UK, but I don't recall receiving an update. Too bad the description wasn't more precise. Was it a non-terrestrial or possibly a manifested entity? I also wonder if this person still has bizarre encounters and/or dreams.

––––––––––

ON MARCH 4, 2019 I received a telephone call from an experiencer who has lived in the Fort Worth, TX area his entire life. 'GF' decided it was time to come forward with his experiences, since he had many questions. He has endured physical encounters, beginning at age eight. GF is now sixty-one and he continues to experience regular visitations by other entities, orbs and craft.

It began when GF was a boy. He started to experience waking paralysis events. This terrified him but would usually end after a few minutes. Then one particular night, he woke in his bed while lying on his back; completely paralyzed. He had no sensations or feeling throughout his body but was totally awake and able to watch what was going on around him. Standing over him were several unknown humanoids that he described as seven to eight feet in height with large upside-down teardrop shaped heads and black almond shaped eyes. There were no other facial features. The skin was medium brown in color and had a smooth texture. The arms were quite thin and long, ending with small hands and three long digits. He was unable to tell what they were doing to him since he had no touch sensation and felt no pain. GL remembers that he had eight to ten of these encounters between the ages of eight and thirty-one.

Each following morning, he would wake with bruises on his arms, legs and chest. He soon noticed a hard, circular object under the skin of his upper right arm. The object remained in his arm until he was a young adult and married. He eventually removed the object himself with the help of his wife. The implant was circular and about the same circumference and thickness of a quarter. It was completely black in color, very hard, smooth and polished. He continues to have an indentation on his arm from where the implant was removed. His wife was frightened by the object and disposed of it, which GL now wishes she had kept. He also stated that, to this day, a clear gel-like substance will occasionally ooze from the indentation. He has been scared to bring up the subject with a physician.

About thirty years ago, GF began to see dark shadowy masses. These masses would manifest at home and at work; any time or place. This phenomenon continues. He would also observe large white orbs float over his house and experience ten foot V-shaped craft hover above him while he was in his yard. Many times, other people or friends, who were with GF, would see the same thing. He states that this will occur maybe once per year and always during daylight.

GF also states that his father and brother have experienced otherworldly encounters as well but refuse to discuss it. GF is fearful that his children and grandchildren are also having similar incidents but reluctant to bring up the subject with them.

I told him that he should open up about his past with them; to see if they follow up with any details. As well, I told him that I would be willing to talk to them if they had questions. The stigma and fear of coming forward about non-terrestrial encounters and abduction needs to be curtailed. *Lon*

6

FEW WORDS CAN DESCRIBE

IN JANUARY 2010, I received an email from a new mother. The following narration is from my initial report and the follow-up information that I received:

> *"I received a rather mysterious email from a woman (I'll refer to her as 'Lisa') who had a traumatic experience recently. Lisa didn't place much content in the email and attached a telephone number, so I called Lisa the next morning. I attempted to write down notes as best as I could; she was very distraught. She gave me permission to post her account anonymously. I will state that she lives on the US west coast.*
>
> *Two months ago, Lisa gave birth to a baby boy. She never mentioned anything about the child's father, but I assumed by some of her comments that she was not in a relationship. Her pregnancy was uneventful though, the OB/GYN insisted that she remain at home for the last trimester. The reason he gave was that Lisa was slightly built and it would be better safe than sorry. She lived with her mother and sister so there was someone usually there to watch over her.*
>
> *In those last months of her pregnancy, the OB/GYN told*

her he and a nurse would come to her mother's home for her exams instead of her coming to his office. She didn't give it much thought at the time but did recognize that this was a bit unusual. The exams were not anything out of the ordinary except for one occasion when the nurse gave her an injection of a 'mild sedative' to relax her during a cervical exam.

I asked her what had happened during that exam and she whispered; "I don't know." Lisa had fallen asleep or was under strong sedation but only remembers the nurse applying a cold compress to her forehead just before they got ready to leave. She said that she thinks that the examination lasted almost a full hour from what she could recollect about the time of day. I asked if her mother and sister were home, but she said that both were at work that day.

In early November 2009, Lisa gave birth to a 6lbs. 8oz baby boy at her local hospital. The labor and birth went easier than she had expected. Her contractions lasted about 10 hours, but she said it was more bearable than she had imagined it would be (this was her first child). The procedure was performed naturally without any pain medication though she said that she did suffer a slight infection a few days later which required her to remain in the hospital for 2 extra days. Her OB/GYN performed the delivery and the nurse who had come to her home was also present.

Everything was fine with the child and Lisa. She had taken the baby to another OB/GYN because her regular doctor was on a 'long vacation.' So, another doctor in his clinic was taking care of his patients until he returned.

A few days before the New Year, Lisa was feeding her child when she noticed that the baby's eyes were a dark, almost violet color instead of the normal blue hue. She said that the baby acted fine, but she called the doctor's office anyway. She was told that infants' eye color can change fairly quickly, and it was nothing to worry about; it was just part of the growing process. After a few days, the child's eyes seemed to lighten some.

It was late morning on New Year's Eve and Lisa was at home alone because her mother and sister were at a friend's wedding. She was in the living room when the baby started to suddenly scream; like it was being hurt. Lisa picked him up and noticed that his eyes were very dark violet but seemed to shine when the baby blinked. The baby continued to scream, but then stopped on a dime. The child's eyes opened wide, looked directly at her and blinked SIDEWAYS! Membranes came across both eyes from the corners and blinked like, in her words, "A lizard."

I asked Lisa to continue her story. She said she immediately called the doctor's office and was told to go to the hospital since the doctor was on call. When the baby was examined, it was determined he was fine and that there was nothing wrong with the eyes. Then Lisa inquired to the emergency room doctor about her regular OB/GYN. She was told that someone would get back to her on that question.

About a half hour later, the OB/GYN who was on call and had filled in for her regular doctor came to the examination room. She looked at the exam reports and stated that everything was fine. Then Lisa was told, in a matter-of-fact manner, that her regular OB/GYN had quit his practice. Lisa asked about his attending nurse. The doctor looked at her like she was crazy and said, "What nurse?" She described the nurse and was told that no one of that description worked at the clinic or the hospital.

Since that day, Lisa says her child's eyes are a light violet color and that she has not noticed the strange side-to-side blinking at all but swears there is something wrong. The child looks at her in a strange manner, with very wide eyes; then *slowly closes his eyes and gives her an unsettling 'smile.' She said she has investigated the OB/GYN and has found that he was licensed to practice but is not anywhere to be found. She told me, "There are few words to describe how I feel."*

In the meantime, I began to wonder if I was having my leg pulled. After some checking, Lisa is actually who she said she was. All of the information I was given was true. I did ask her why she contacted me and was told that I was 'referred' to her and that I could give her some idea where to go. I gave her some contact addresses and links as well as assurance that I would remain available if she needed to contact me.

My last question to Lisa was; "What do you think is going on?" As I expected, she tells me her theory of reptilians and alien hybrids; and that the OB/GYN and nurse may be aliens, etc. I'm not discounting any of her thoughts. But as with every other incident or case I've researched, I'm not taking all the information as fact. I truly believe Lisa is sincere and I will continue to keep in touch with her. But, in the meantime, I'll continue with an open and somewhat skeptical mind. Lon

ON MONDAY, January 2, 2012, I received the following email from Lisa:

"Lon, I hope you had a very nice holiday. You had asked me to contact you if there was any notable information concerning my son and me. He is doing well and is very healthy. My mother has remarked that he is the healthiest baby she has ever seen because he does not catch colds or exhibit other minor ailments, including fevers. In fact, his pediatrician has also remarked about his clean medical record but has not

mentioned it as a problem, but I am concerned because this just does not seem right to me.

We moved into an apartment a few months ago. He goes to daycare on some days and stays with my mother on others. We have all noticed a strange characteristic that he has exhibited for the past year or so. Sometimes he will sit on the floor with his arms folded and stare straight ahead for up to ten minutes. I've noticed that his eyes will turn a darker shade of violet during these episodes. He doesn't make any noise and is almost impossible to rouse. Afterwards he acts like he has been zapped of his energy and will occasionally take a brief nap. Have you heard of this type of activity before?

I made you aware of my thoughts on alien involvement during our first conversation. I honestly don't know what you think about that. Since then I had thought less of that theory but now, I'm wondering if there was some type of intervention. I have still not been able to contact the OB/GYN who suddenly left his practice. The AMA has no further record of him practicing anywhere. Now I'm starting to be wary of the pediatrician which, I agree, is somewhat paranoid.

As before, if you or others you know could offer reassurance, I would be very grateful."

I contacted Lisa by telephone the next day. She was at her office so she may have been more discreet than before. Her demeanor was quite uneasy. She was very concerned that something was seriously amiss in relation to her son's physical and mental well-being. She was also worried that some procedure may have been performed on her during the time she was sedated while pregnant. She had a few odd physical changes that I was asked not to describe; at least for now. She had promised to keep me in the loop, though I felt that she needed to come forward in order to receive extensive medical treatment.

She continued to maintain that her family and I were the only parties with knowledge of her identification and situation.

ON JANUARY 15, 2013, I received another email update from
Lisa:

"Hello Lon, I hope you are doing well. I have been receiving your email newsletter daily and enjoy it.

My situation has changed since I last wrote you. We now live outside Los Angeles, CA. My son is now three years old and attends pre-school though it has been difficult because he refuses to join activities that involve the other children. He'd rather sit by himself and draw or read. His reading level has been tested at 3rd grade level and is very accomplished at drawing. He has the ability to draw almost perfect straight lines and circles.

He was being seen by a psychologist who said that he is anti-social, possibly a savant. I totally disagree with this assessment and have decided to have him tested at a local university. The testing includes a full physical evaluation which has me a bit worried. I'm scared that something unusual will be discovered that may lead to more intensive examination. I'm probably be paranoid, but I am concerned.

As before he occasionally sits on the floor with his arms folded and stares directly ahead for up to a half hour at a time. I've noticed that his eyes still turn a darker shade of violet, but it doesn't last for more than a few minutes. He doesn't make any noise and it is impossible to get attention during these periods. Afterwards he takes a brief nap. This only happens at home. The pre-school staff has never mentioned this behavior.

If you get a chance, there are a few things I'd like to ask you by phone, not for public consumption. I don't mind you publishing this because I want your readers to offer advice. I look forward to talking to you."

I called Lisa a day or so later and we discussed a few other odd incidents. I personally felt that Lisa's son may have been influenced by 'others' though I didn't want to get too deep into that subject with Lisa until she had her son examined.

Unfortunately, I never heard back from Lisa since the January 2013 conversation. I made several attempts to contact her, including inquiries to her mother and her job. No one would offer me any additional information, which was quite odd. Had the incident actually occurred, or was I being played? I truly feel that this was a true set of incidents; but I can't imagine what had happened to her and her son.

A WOMAN NAMED Delia provided a Puerto Rican research group the following account, which was later forwarded to me:

"One day during the month of October, a friend and I were at a Yoga Center. In this place various yoga activities are celebrated and also people go there to meditate. It was 7:30 p.m. when my friend and I decided to retire and go to sleep.

Then, all of a sudden somebody put their hand on my face. I couldn't see who it was because the room was dark. I was then suspended in the air, flying towards a direction that was totally unknown to me. While I was being transported in the air, I could see houses and trees below me. At that moment I was so scared that I couldn't move, speak or scream.

I calculate that the time had elapsed while I was being

transported was approximately from 7:30 p.m. to 5:00 a.m. I was in my room when I woke up at 5:00 a.m. Immediately, I started vomiting and all my body was in terrible pain.

After a while, I felt a little better and I went to talk to the director of the Yoga Center. I told him how terrible I felt and what had happened to me. He told me to go back to my room and sleep until 12:00 noon and that when I woke up, I would feel much better. I followed his advice.

After this I was left with a strange sensation which is difficult to explain. One of the sensations was in my vaginal (area), the other was in my mind; my way of thinking. Before I didn't give too much importance to the simple things that surrounded me, but I suddenly began to notice how beautiful the sky was and also feeling a great amount of love towards other people. In other words, my life had changed completely.

Time passed by and it was already December; three months after my extraordinary experience. During these three months, I had noticed that my period occurred every fifty days, not every twenty-seven days, or so, as would normally happen. Also, my stomach had enlarged just a little. Time passed by and then I had another encounter with a UFO.

Suddenly, I found myself in a metallic room where there were twelve small men (not human) all dressed in grey. In this room I was lying in a metallic bed where I can clearly remember giving birth to a child. It was a normal vaginal birth, though my two other children had been born by Cesarean. Then suddenly I fell asleep. When I woke, I saw one of the extraterrestrials with a child in his arms.

When I saw this child something deep inside of me told me he was my child, but I also remember being afraid. I remember telling one of the extraterrestrials that I considered this child strange, because he was half human and half extraterrestrial!

Also, I can remember telling myself that even though this

child was strange I had to accept and love him because he was my child. Also, the way he looked at me and the expression on his face confirmed this to me. After a moment, the extraterrestrial brought the child to me so that I could hold him.

Even though I know he belongs to me, I cannot have him. And, because of this, my pain and sorrow cannot go away. They told me that he could not live with me because he could not eat the food that we human beings eat. While I held him in my arms, I didn't want to let him go. I held him very tight. Then the extraterrestrials took him away from me and escorted me to the entrance of the craft.

After these two experiences, I have had two more children. The other two occurred when they brought me the child so that I could be with him. They do so by transporting me by air, holding the child in my arms.

While I am being transported, I have noticed that they conduct a certain experiment with me. I remember feeling fear, like if the child would just fall right out of my arms. I suppose that they do this to see how human mother's instincts are towards their children.

At the present, my two children have also had UFO experiences. They both have developed a certain high degree of mental abilities and presently are being studied by them. I can't help worrying that probably one of these days my children can also be abducted."

This is a sentiment I have heard from other mothers and fathers who believe they have hybrid children or offspring that have been influenced by otherworldly beings.

HUMANOID RESEARCHER ALBERT S. Rosales provided an account from New South Wales, Australia:

"The witness, John, was driving back from Lismore when his car suddenly stopped. He checked under the hood but could not find anything obvious, so he decided to start walking to get help. John stated that he had a strange feeling like something was touching his spine. He looked up to see two bright white lights about five hundred meters above him and heard what he described as like the sound of an arc welder.

He noticed that there were trucks driving by on the road. John then hit the ground and rolled down the embankment. He then noticed a Grey alien, which said to him; "You can't get away" and grabbed him by the arm and proceeded towards one of the motherships. John stated that the craft was shaped like the Egyptian 'Eye of Osiris,' metallic and gunmetal gray with no apparent openings. He said that both walked straight through the wall.

The alien (who John learned his name was Theoraba) took him inside and observed other aliens working on computers, etc. He also noticed small beings in flasks of red-orange solution. John asked Theoraba; "What are those?" Theoraba replied that they were 'babies.' Theoraba then asked him; "Would you like to have something to do with these in the future?" Two aliens then grabbed his arms and legs as he was approached by a female alien who he thought was a human 'hybrid.' She had the body of a human woman, long arms, five fingers and very dark black eyes. He was told that the aliens wanted him to father children for them, and at this point John began to panic.

The female alien then took on a more human appearance as he then became sexually aroused and had intercourse with the female alien. A metal object was later introduced into his anal cavity and a patch of skin from his left palm was taken. When he asked about the skin sample, he was told that their planet had disintegrated. In order to continue their species and ensure that genetic inbreeding didn't occur that hybrids were the only alternative.

That same year on another occasion John was walking along the road at Kingscliffe and saw two motherships again and shouted at them to leave him alone. Apparently, he met the now familiar gray alien who told him that they had inserted an implant in his finger.

On another occasion while in the bush, John encountered a female alien hybrid, which he assumes was one of his offspring. He communicated with her telepathically. He states that she was quite young and because of this was wearing what he assumed to be a breathing apparatus, which went from around her head into her mouth and nostrils. He was told that she was unable to breathe in our atmosphere. John claims he has bred five male and one female hybrid offspring."

THIS ACCOUNT IS similar to the well-known historical account of Brazilian farmer Antonio Villas Boas, who claimed to have been abducted by extraterrestrials for breeding purposes on October 16, 1957 near Sao Francisco de Salles in Minas Gerais, Brazil. The 23-year-old Brazilian farmer was working in the early morning darkness to avoid the hot temperatures of the day.

As he was plowing a field, he saw what he described as a 'red star' in the sky. According to Antonio, this star approached him, growing in size until it became recognizable as a roughly circular or egg-shaped craft, with a red light at its front and a rotating dome on top. The craft began descending to land in the field, extending three legs as it did so. At that point, Boas decided to leave.

According to Boas, he first attempted to leave the scene on his tractor, but when its lights and engine died after traveling only a short distance, he decided to continue on foot. However, he was seized by a five-foot tall humanoid, who was wearing grey coveralls and a helmet. Its eyes were small and blue, and instead of speech it made noises like barks or yelps. Three similar beings then joined the first in subduing Boas, and they dragged him inside their craft.

Once inside the craft, Boas said that he was stripped of his clothes and covered from head-to-toe with a strange gel. He was then led into a large semicircular room, through a doorway that had strange red symbols written over it. In this room the beings took samples of Boas' blood from his chin. After this he was then taken to a third room and left alone for around half an hour. During this time, some kind of gas was pumped into the room, which made Boas become violently ill.

Shortly after, Boas claimed that he was joined in the room by another humanoid. This one, however, was female, very attractive, and naked. She was the same height as the other beings he had encountered, with a small, pointed chin and large, blue catlike eyes. The hair on her head was long and white but her underarm and pubic hair were bright red. Boas said he was strongly attracted to the woman, and the two had sexual intercourse. During this act, Boas noted that the female did not kiss him but instead nipped him on the chin and, like the others he had encountered, made barking noises instead of speech.

When it was over, the female smiled at Boas, rubbing her belly and gestured upwards. Boas took this to mean that she was going to raise their child in space. The female seemed relieved that their 'task' was over, and Boas himself said that he felt angered by the situation, because he felt as though he had been little more than 'a good stallion' for the humanoids.

Boas said that he was then given back his clothing and taken on a tour of the ship by the humanoids. During this tour he said that he attempted to take a clock-like device as proof of his encounter but was caught by the humanoids and prevented from doing so. He was then escorted off the ship and watched as it took off, glowing brightly. When Boas returned home, he discovered that four hours had passed. There has been a lot of doubt expressed about Boas' encounter, but overall, the scenario is similar to other claims by experiencers. Boas' abduction and sexual descriptions were quite unusual for that time period and Ufology was in its infancy.

―――――

"And it came to pass, when men began to multiply on the face of the Earth, and daughters were being born unto them, that the sons of God saw the daughters of men that they were fair, and they took them wives of all which they chose." – Genesis 6:2

COULD this verse be interpreted as extraterrestrials visited Earth and mated with early Homo subspecies or Homo Neanderthal females, in order to sire the modern human race of Homo Sapiens?

MARIA RIVERA'S EXPERIENCER ACCOUNT

THE FOLLOWING information was forwarded to me by experiencer Maria M. Rivera of Aguada, Puerto Rico. This case was previous to my involvement in the David Eckhart family home infestation and abductions. Mrs. Rivera was unable to convince UFO reporting agencies to investigate her experiences until I started to report on the incidents. Since that time, there have been several reports of UFOs in the rainforests in and around the area of Aguada and other municipalities located in the western coastal valley region bordering the Atlantic Ocean:

"Submitted herein is this UFO sighting/alien encounter story which occurred here in Aguada, Puerto Rico (a US territory). This alien encounter and subsequent abduction was reported to several UFO/extraterrestrial investigator websites. However, it was so frightening that it reminded me of a horror story. We had to abandon our house after we bought it in August 2005, because no investigator came to help us, and recently sold the house to move away from that rainforest. The following information was reported, however, included after

that are additional occurrences that were not reported to any other websites before and which occurred after May 1, 2006.

On November 10, 2005, at approximately 3:00 a.m., my daughter and I heard a weird humming sound like a hurricane wind going by my house. The sound was so strange that penetrated our ears. When my daughter and I looked outside, we observed what appeared to be a disc-shaped object moving westward towards the rear of the house where an enormous rainforest and a huge antenna are located, which leads all the way to the Atlantic Ocean. The disc was silver in color with a row of windows around it and had a greenish haze or aura covering the craft. All the windows appeared to be a darker green color. The craft appeared to be descending as though it was about to land somewhere behind the house. We lived in Brooklyn, New York near Kennedy Airport for over twenty years and the airplanes flew low over my house twenty-four hours a day. I know what we have seen and the sound it made was something very unusual, something we've never heard or seen before. After that, my daughter and I heard the same sound at least twice a week. I used to go to sleep at 3:00 a.m. after watching novellas.

On Friday, April 28, 2006, at approximately 3:00 a.m., I heard again the same sound going by my house. At about ten or fifteen minutes later I heard my dog (Dora) barking continuously in my backyard. When I went to investigate by turning on the backyard light (the light in the house was off) and by looking through my dining room window, I observed my dog lying on her back with her four legs up apparently unconscious. The dog was chained to a metal pole next to the back fence which separates my property with the rainforest in the back. I called her name; "Dora, Dora, what's wrong Dora?" But she did not respond. When I lifted my eyes and looked at the back fence, which is about twenty-five feet from where I was standing, I observed two creatures (extraterrestrials) standing close to and behind the chain-link fence looking at me. One of the aliens was about three feet from the dog and the other alien was about five feet away from the other alien. They were about three and a half feet tall with a large oval head and big black slanted eyes. They had pale grayish skin and a barely visible slit for a mouth and two little holes for a nose. They also had very skinny arms and they seem not to have any clothes on. Their legs were not showing because under the fence there was a cinder-block wall about one and a half feet high. I could only see them from the waist up.

The aliens were staring at me and I was staring at them. I think that they were communicating with me telepathically because they were reading my mind when I said mentally; "I'm going to wake up my husband, Nelson." I left the window and walked through the hallway leading to the bedrooms. On the way to wake up my husband, they detoured me to the other bedroom to wake up my daughter instead. I woke up my daughter (17-years-old at the time) and both of us went to the dining room window where we observed the creatures still standing in the same place. Again, they stared at us and we stared straight into their large black eyes for a while. My daughter said to me; "Mommy, I'm going back to bed because I'm scared, then I won't be able to sleep." I then followed my daughter to the bedroom because she was afraid to go by herself. Approximately 10 minutes later I returned to the dining room window, the aliens were still there in the same location. While staring straight into their big black eyes, the one closest to the dog was telling me in my mind to open the door leading to the backyard. I said in my mind; "I'm not going to open the door." He demanded telepathically; "You're going to open the door." I then felt myself moving towards the door and was getting drowsy.

I don't remember what happened after that. I woke up in my bed. I asked my daughter if she had seen the same thing, in case I was imagining things. She described the incident and the creatures the same way and manner I described them. We then told my husband who slept in a separate bedroom facing the backyard. He slept there because my daughter was afraid to sleep by herself, so I had to sleep with her. My husband stated that he did hear the dog barking wildly at about 3:00 a.m. He said that he looked out the bedroom window, without getting off the bed, since the bed was against the window. He saw the dog barking towards the rainforest in the back but thought that she was barking at a cat. He stated that he did not look at the fence or the rainforest and was so tired that he immediately went back to sleep.

Please be advised that behind the back fence, where the aliens were, is an enormous rainforest that leads all the way to the Atlantic Ocean, where a huge antenna is located and is pitch black at night. I later found out that the antenna and the land where it sits are federal property and the area is fenced in.

What concerns me the most is that my husband informed me that he discovered the back door opened when he got up at about 8:00 in the morning but did not know what happened. My daughter informed me that she opened her eyes about 5:00 in the morning and did not find me next to her in bed. She thought I was in the bathroom or somewhere around the house and went back to sleep. The dog did not want to eat or drink anything for days and was lying down apparently sick.

On Monday, May 1, 2006, at about 12:50 a.m., while sitting in the living room and while talking on the phone, I saw a bright light, like an enormous light bulb, moving through the rainforest. I informed my husband and we immediately closed all the louver windows in the kitchen and dining room. I became hysterical and began to cry because I *thought that they were after me and my husband had to calm me down.*

At approximately 2:00 a.m., the same night, I heard the same sound again over the house. Seconds later, while lying in bed, my husband and I heard a loud crashing noise like something hitting the flat concrete roof and shook the house like if something had landed there. We were afraid but did not call the police for fear of being ridiculed and not come to investigate. It was such a terrifying experience that we didn't even consider going outside and check it out. Instead the three of us huddled in one bed.

I feel relieved to know that I was not the only one seeing those alien beings. My 17-year-old daughter saw them too. Otherwise I, myself, would think that I was hallucinating and imagining things. Could it be possible that I did open the backyard door and was abducted by the aliens? I don't know, my husband found the back door opened early in the morning. In addition, I have dotted puncture marks on my left hand which is circular and had a slight burning pain which diminished as time went by since April 28, 2006. Although faded it is still visible, especially when observed in person, after almost two years. We moved from New York City and bought that house in August 2005 when my husband retired as an Assistant Deputy Warden after working for 20 years for the New York City Department of Correction (Riker's Island jail complex) and after having a heart attack. I am a serious woman who doesn't like to lie. I never thought that we would go through something like that. But what my daughter and I saw and what my husband and I heard is the truth. Never in my life did I believe in UFOs or aliens. I never cared, seen, read or even heard anything about how they look until we witnessed the unexplained here on the island. We moved to another house that we own in Aguada which is pretty far from the beach and that rainforest. And my daughter was so traumatized that we sent her to live with my sister in Stroudsburg, Pennsylvania. Since we sold that house, we're planning to sell the other one to return to the US mainland because I fear they're after me.

Several days after our encounter with the alien beings, on May 9, 2006, at approximately 1:00 p.m., we went to see Mr. Luis A. Echevarria, the mayor of Aguada. We were informed that he was not at City Hall but attending a meeting in San Juan. We instead notified Mr. Martin Concepcion, who works for Puerto Rico's Civil Defense Agency in Aguada and handed him a written copy of the incident. He stated that he will investigate, will put a request to the Municipal Police to patrol the area and will make a copy for the mayor. He also stated that he will get back to us, but he never did.

On May 11, 2006, at approximately 11:00 a.m., we went to the channel 5 television network located in the city of Mayaguez. At the television network, we were interviewed by a young man who stated that here in Puerto Rico people are superstitious or when they report that they saw a UFO/extraterrestrial it is later dismissed as a hoax. My husband and I were so upset, we told him that we are 'Nuyoricans' therefore not superstitious and just because someone lied, doesn't mean that we are liars.

We even sent emails to several Puerto Rican UFO investigative organizations, but they didn't email us back. We did not know who to turn to since we were not getting help from anyone here on the island. So, my husband and I started sending emails to the US mainland to see whether someone or some organization would help us. We are not seeking publicity but the truth."

After I gained Maria's trust, she began to confide in me by

offering further details of her encounters. The following information was forwarded to me exclusively:

*"On June 5, 2006, at approximately 3:00 a.m., after watching
television, I proceeded to the kitchen to get a glass of milk
before going to bed. As I walked through the living room on my
way to the bedroom, I observed an alien peeping through the
glass-pane window on the main entrance door. Outside that
door is a balcony and obviously, he was standing on top of a
patio chair next to the door, because being a short creature, he
couldn't reach the high window on the door. This one really
scared me a lot because he looked older, meaner and had a
mark on his forehead. The two aliens I saw behind the fence in
my backyard looked like little kids with a serene look on their
face. But not this one, he had a sinister evil look on his face. I
hurried to my husband's bedroom, woke him up. He grabbed a
machete in case it was an intruder, and proceeded out to the
balcony, but no one was around. Could this alien be their
leader?*

*On October 22, 2006, at approximately 11:00 p.m. there
was a three-hour blackout in the town of Aguada. At
approximately 1200 a.m., I awoke my husband so he could
hear a weird humming sound coming from behind the house
in the rainforest. The backyard and surrounding rainforest
were pitch black when we went out with flashlights to listen
closely. I called my sister on the cellphone so she could hear
the weird sound coming from the woods, but suddenly we got
frightened and hurried back inside the house.*

*On February 25, 2007, at approximately 4:00 a.m., I
was in my bedroom which faces the front of the house. I
looked through the window and observed a disc-shaped craft,
similar to the one my daughter and I saw previously,
hovering motionless about 40 meters from the house and*

about forty meters from the ground. The craft was about thirty feet in diameter. It was so low and so close that I was able to observe curious extraterrestrials watching me and the house through viewing ports surrounding the craft. They were silhouetting through the bright greenish blue background and appeared very inquisitive looking out the windows. I also observed that they were passing a long rod to one another. My immediate reaction at the moment was that it may have been a telescope or some other device. Unlike the others I've seen and heard, this craft was hovering silently. The whole event probably lasted about a minute. I ran to my husband's bedroom and woke him up. He immediately grabbed the camcorder next to his bed. Unfortunately, by the time we got to the window, the UFO was nowhere in sight.

On May 21, 2007, at approximately 1:00 a.m. my daughter was on her cellphone in the living room by herself talking to her friends in New York. The lights in the living room were off except for a dim light on a table lamp. Suddenly she heard the humming sound again and a greenish blue light flashing through all the windows. This light flashed in sequence starting from the front windows to the back windows. It looked like something had flown low by heading towards the back of the house. My daughter screamed and ran to the bedroom where she was shaking in fear. It may have been nothing, but it showed that she was traumatized after what she had seen on November 10, 2005 and April 28, 2006.

My 21-year-old son came to visit us from New York. On June 2, 2007, at approximately 2:00 am, he explained that while in his bedroom, which is located downstairs, a very bright beam of green light shone through the window and through the glass-pane door lighting up the whole bedroom for a few seconds. He was so frightened that after the light vanished, he hysterically ran upstairs in his pajamas to inform us. He refused to sleep in that bedroom again.

On August 14, 2007, early in the morning, we noticed that our dog, Dora, was gone. We do not know if she had come loose and ran away. We do have a high fence that goes around our property and the dog was kept chained overnight, so I don't see how that's possible. We looked all over our neighborhood, we asked our neighbors if they had seen her. We even searched throughout the town of Aguada, but to no avail. I do not know if it had something to do with those aliens, but after what happened to me and my family in that house, anything for me is possible. We moved soon afterwards to our other house.

In this house where we live now, on November 3, 2007, at approximately 2:00 a.m., while in bed before I fell asleep, I saw a small blueish green neon light, about the size of a penny, coming from the window, moving through the bedroom in the dark. I became paralyzed while looking at it. Suddenly my bed was being surrounded with those creatures. Obviously, I was made unconscious because when I opened my eyes, I found myself naked in a different cold room and lying face-up on very cold 'stainless steel' platform. This platform seemed to be floating on the air without legs or anything supporting it. It was narrow enough that each arm hanged on each side. Still feeling paralyzed but conscious they commenced injecting me with a long needle or something. I begged them with my thoughts, to please not to do it, but they ignored me. I also felt that they put something metallic, like a round suction cup about five inches in diameter, on the right side of my abdomen. It felt like my flesh was being stretched and my inside was being sucked out like a powerful vacuum. I was in excruciating pain when they did that, but I was unable to scream or move.

About five or six creatures surrounded the platform, one

being taller than the others and the rest were the short Greys I previously seen in my backyard. This time they were not communicating telepathically among themselves because I heard a weird incoherent mumbling sound coming from them. However, I didn't see their mouths move. I remember calling them 'Marcianos' (Martians), they revealed telepathically, in Spanish, that they don't like being called Martians, but preferred to be called 'creatures.'

When I woke in my bed the next morning, I still had pain on the right side of my abdomen, but no mark was visible. Since my daughter doesn't sleep with me anymore because she now lives in Pennsylvania, I now sleep with my husband. He keeps telling me to wake him up when it happens, but I could not move or speak. Many times, he stays awake late at night in bed, but nothing happens so he falls asleep. I do, however, feel or have a sense when they're around.

At this point, it is important to be note that I've had ovarian cancer and have had several operations to remove parts of my intestine. I also received several operations for breast cancer. I flew occasionally to New York City to see my private doctors since here on the island private doctors are reluctant to accept Blue Cross and Blue Shield or GHI which I got from my husband's retirement. I was informed by my doctors in New York that the cancer had returned and that I urgently needed another operation. I used to be in constant stomach pain and noticed blood in my stool and urine when I went to the bathroom. It was not the first time the cancer has recurred before and they operated on me after each recurrence. But after the encounter with those creatures on April 28, 2006, I returned to New York. Several tests were performed, and no cancer was detected. The pain and the bleeding had stopped. I truly feel that those creatures had cured me. What is my opinion of the creatures? I sincerely believe that they're benevolent and compassionate creatures, but I'm afraid of them. They do not have my permission to do with my body whatever they please. Although I believe they have cured me, I am not their guinea pig.

I have something in my right lower back that has been bugging me for a long time. It moves when I touch it and I know it was not there before. I saw on the History Channel the program called UFO Hunters when Mr. Bill Birnes took a man who was abducted by a UFO to Dr. Roger Leir. The man had an alien implant in his leg. When Dr. Leir put a powerful magnet where the man had the implant, to our amazement, the object inside his flesh moved towards the magnet and the skin bulged. Like that man, I don't have an entry wound or a scar where the object is. That prompted me and my husband to do the same experiment. Unfortunately, we do not have a powerful magnet like the one used by Dr. Leir. The mark on my left hand and the object on my back have been noticed by me since my encounter with those aliens on April 28, 2006.

We recently learned that here in Puerto Rico this type of phenomenon occurs all over the island, especially in El Yunque rainforest where people get lost for days and come back with incredible stories. El Yunque is the only tropical rainforest in the United States National Forest System. Could there be an extraterrestrial base in the El Yunque rainforest? Could there be an extraterrestrial base in the woods behind my property or somewhere in the Atlantic Ocean? Since the town of Aguada is situated in the northwest corner of the island, could that be a route for UFOs to fly towards the Bermuda Triangle? My daughter and I did hear a weird humming sound very often and very close to the house. The craft we observed on November 10, 2005 appeared to be descending as though it was about to land somewhere behind my house. Let me reiterate, we lived in Brooklyn, New York near Kennedy

Airport for over twenty years and the airplanes flew low over my house twenty-four hours a day. I know what we have seen and the sound it made were something very unusual, something we've never heard or seen before.

I have tried to write a thorough and detailed story to focus attention on what my family and I went through in that house and to demonstrate our reason for moving. What happened to me and my family is no hoax. It was a terrifying experience. To prove this, I am willing to submit to a polygraph test, go under hypnosis, be under oath or whatever. I sincerely say thank you for reading my story and hope for your understanding."

Maria and her family eventually moved back to the United States, and they seem to have avoided further encounters. Before they left Puerto Rico, Maria was able to capture video footage of a disc-shaped craft descending into the rainforest. She wrote to me soon after this:

"Dear Lon - per your request, I do have one more thing to show you.

Enclosed herein is a recording of a saucer-shaped object for your observation and analysis to supplement the UFO sightings and subsequent alien abduction story you have on your website.

On June 11, 2008, at approximately 2:52 a.m., I was alone in the living room when I suddenly got a feeling that I should go outside onto the balcony and there it was again. My camcorder was not in the immediate area, but luckily, I had my cellphone with me. It appeared to be a saucer-shaped object, similar to the UFOs I've seen previously, with lights around it. It was hovering motionless.

Listen carefully at the background noise. You can hear the crickets chirping mixed with the sound that the object is making. The sound is similar to the other UFOs I've seen before. It was over the wooded mountains near the other house I moved to.

The reason why I send it to you now was because it was recorded on my cellphone. I recorded the object for approximately fifteen seconds before I feared to be alone on the balcony and in the dark.

Thank you for your attention." Maria

I was given permission to send the video to a few trustworthy associates for their opinion. After several extensive tests and later observations in the area of the sighting, the conclusion was that the video was authentic.

_____

8

REPTILIANS / SAURIAN ENCOUNTERS

WHAT ARE THE REPTILIANS? These 'lizard people' are also referred to as 'Saurians,' 'Draconians,' or 'Reptoids.' Some researchers describe them as ancient shapeshifting humanoids that have inhabited Earth before the time of man. Others believe that these beings come from a royal extraterrestrial lineage that currently dominates world governments and financial markets. There are also claims that the Anunnaki, who were supposedly a winged Draconian race, descended into Mesopotamia during the fourth century BCE with the knowledge of the planets in the solar system, the precession of the equinoxes, and an understanding of complex medical procedures. It has also been said that the Anunnaki gave the Sumerians a 'stargate' before leaving Earth.

I'm not going to make any argument as to the identity of these entities or if they actually existed in antiquity, but I do know that their presence is mentioned in many experiencer encounter and abduction accounts.

_____

IN DECEMBER 2011, I began an exchange of emails with an Austrian geologist named Gregor. There were some communication difficulties that needed to be ironed out since his written English was an issue. After a month or so, Gregor agreed to the final version of his encounter:

"Hello Lon - I am writing to you from where I live in Gmunden, Austria. Recently I came across your story about the man who had an encounter with an alien type creature in a cave in the United States. The story is similar to my encounter in an obscure cave here in Upper Austria. This area is known for salt mining and Salzkammergut, the salt mines of the former Habsburg empire. I am a trained and certified geologist. I studied at the University of Salzburg and in the United States at the University of Wisconsin, Madison. I have explored and documented cave systems throughout Austria, Czech Republic and Poland since 1988. In May 2011, I was in a narrow cave that a colleague had recently found. This was approximately 2 KM north of Obertraun on the opposite side of the descending mountain range in the foothills near the east bank of Halsatter See (lake). As I moved through the difficult passageway, I started to hear voices emanating from the darkness ahead of me. I stopped to collect a few samples from the cave wall; chipping it with my pick. I moved deeper, maybe 50 meters, until I noticed the voices again. I am familiar with echoes and Doppler effect sounds in caves, but this was totally different. I stood quietly for several minutes until the voices stopped.

Again, I moved through the cave, almost crawling at this point. After another 40 meters I ascended into a chamber that was big enough to accommodate several people. There were two wide openings on the opposite side of the chamber. Each looked like it had been excavated by machine. There was also an obvious rotting odor. As I examined the chamber, I noticed an odd red iridescence as I passed the light over the rock floor. When I knelt down to collect a sample, I again heard voices coming from one of the passageways. At this point I was terrified and started to hurry back through the narrow cave. After I squeezed back several meters, I was able to turn my head just enough to look back into the dark chamber.

A yellow light slowly made its way into the chamber from the left opening in the chamber. Then there were several yellow lights following the first. As the lights moved through the opening into the chamber then back through the opening on the right, I was able to see the beings. The sight sent fear throughout my body. I was actually paralyzed.

The creatures were humanoid in stature; but these were not humans. Each varied in height but all looked the same. Muscular lizards that walked upright like humans. There is not a better term I can use to identify these beings. These creatures wore dark colored full-body uniforms that extended and covered the feet. I couldn't tell the exact color of the skin, but each had a pronounced muzzle. The long tails were very prominent and swiftly swayed back and forth as they moved forward. The arms and legs were massive. I could detect the musculature through the tight uniforms. There were voices also; as if they were talking to each other. The voices actually sounded human though I could not detect the language. There were possibly 20 or more of these creatures as they walked single file through the chamber and into the other opening.

When I determined it was safe to move, I quickly withdrew from the cave. I think I may have been in shock because I barely remember anything that happened from that point until I reached my office. I decided to keep a private journal regarding my encounter; but I have not discussed it with anyone else. My colleague who originally found the cave told me that he has explored the cave since my encounter but never mentions anything about the chamber, other passageways or bizarre beings.

At this point in time, I am starting to doubt that I witnessed these creatures. Is it possible that I hallucinated this encounter or possibly experienced something from the past or the future? I am a trained professional who deals with reality, but my beliefs have been seriously shaken. I appreciate your, introspect and thoughts, as well as observation by your readers. Thank you." Gregor

THE FACT that Gregor wondered if his encounter was a scene from another time or reality, he may have answered his own question. Over the years, I have collected personal accounts of cryptids / anomalous encounters in Vietnam and other parts of Indochina. I received a particular narrative that was much different from the others that had been forwarded to me. The post is a compilation of three emails, which included answers to a few of my questions. The man who provided this information was, at the time of the incident, a corporal in the US Army, who had since retired from the military after a lengthy career. He did not give me specifics as to his unit and mission but feels strongly that his experience should be told. He provided two identifica-tion references, which checked out. Overall, this man served a distinguished military career and his reputation is quite admirable from what I have seen. Some of the information has been edited at the request of the witness:

"In 1970, I was serving as a corporal in the US Army; deployed to South Vietnam in a region about thirty miles south of the DMZ. At the time I was second-in-command of a squad

of soldiers. We had setup a bivouac in a jungle area that had a few steep hills. That evening my section was ordered to patrol one of the small valleys west of the encampment. We moved out led by our sergeant.

Not long after entering one of the small valleys we detected movement ahead of us. It seemed to be scattered activity, so we doubted it was VC but we weren't positive. We hunkered down for about fifteen minutes getting occasional glimpses of something moving within the trees and brush. There wasn't enough light to detect what we were observing even though the moonlight was bright that night.

After a while the activity halted, so we continued to move slowly through the valley. As we approached a sheer wall on the hill it looked like someone or something had stacked large stones and boulders in the pass in front of us. There was also an opening in the hill side that looked like a cave entrance; approximately five-foot high and three-foot wide narrowing at the top. When observing the passageway, it appeared to have been cut away by machinery. The edges were smooth with small even-spaced grooves.

We were puzzled by this because we had never seen enemy caves like this, just underground tunnels. The sergeant suggested that it may be a VC supply depot, so we started to assess how we were going to investigate the cave. About this time, things got very strange. We began to notice a putrid odor emanating from the cave entrance. The only thing I can compare it to was rotting eggs and human decay. It was so revolting that a few of the soldiers were becoming ill and started to back away into the jungle, including the sergeant. I was directing a light into the entrance in order to observe anything, but there was a haze that was impossible to see through. We had no idea what was before us.

The entire squad took a position in the heavy brush

approximately one hundred and fifty feet from the entrance; far enough not to be detected but close enough to observe the cave entrance. We quietly remained there for what seemed like forever. The jungle was strangely calm though we heard rumbling sounds coming from the distance. It was really eerie. The sergeant was sitting near me talking to himself. It was obvious that he was frightened. I was looking at the rest of the squad. Each soldier had wide eyes and were scanning the area. No one was going to doze off during this patrol.

After several hours, dawn was approaching, and it started to lighten up. I checked my watch. It was just before 0500 hours. Just then we noticed movement in front of the cave. An unknown being (I first thought it was a man) moved through the entrance into the clearing in front of the cave. As it stood up from a crouching posture it stood at least seven-foot high and started to look in our direction. At that time, another similar-looking creature was moving out of the cave. They were making hellish 'hissing' sounds and looking directly at us. The only way I can describe these beings is that they looked like upright lizards. The scaly, shiny skin was very dark, almost black. Snake-like faces with forward set eyes that were very large. They had arms and legs like a human but with scaly skin. I didn't notice a tail, though they wore long one-piece dark green robes along with a dark cap-like covering on their heads. I never noticed if they had anything on their feet.

No one gave the order. It seemed like the entire squad opened fire at once. Every piece of vegetation between us and them was quickly sheared away. I yelled out a cease-fire order. At the same time, I was looking in the direction of the cave. There was nothing there. We immediately checked our flank in case these things circled around, but there was nothing.

As we approached the cave, ready to resume action if needed, it became apparent that the beings had escaped; most *likely back into the cave. It was soon decided to set charges and close the cave entrance.*

When we returned to camp, we all seemed to be in a daze. There was little discussion of the incident and we were never debriefed. I'm positive the sergeant never filed a report. Then again, if he did, it was kept quiet by the brass." Name Withheld

Like I previously stated, this was one of the strangest war time accounts I have ever read. Even though there was no debrief, I'm sure the soldiers talked amongst themselves; verifying what each had witnessed.

I RECEIVED the next account in the Fall of 2010:

"I awoke one night in a state of which I can only explain as a spasm, my body was in a rigid state. I could not move a muscle. I fought to get movement back in my body. I could not turn my head or move at all. It was like I was having a fight to get control of my body. After a few panic-stricken moments, I could just barely move my fingers, only a little bit. I then felt that there was more than just a spasm. I felt dirty and touched. It was a horrible feeling from deep inside me.

I could barely move my toes, again very slightly. I could feel something was on top of me. My hands where by my side, but it felt like they were around my own throat, holding tightly. I was using all my might to break free from this spasmodic state.

Then I could feel something breathing into my left ear; a sound of a growl-like noise right next to my ear. I struggled to move my head to the left, like breaking free from a strangle hold.

I could barely see the outline of a head, a big long head next to my own face. As the spasm-like feeling started to wear off, a tiny bit at a time, I could work out that this thing on top of me looked like a lizard/newt creature. It was like a blending together of all that was around it, or maybe invisible. I'm not very sure which, but I could see it clearly as the seconds passed on.

It was Reptilian. I growled at it, or I think I did. My mind and my body gave all it could to do so. I bared my teeth at it, and I could feel it could read my mind. I was swearing at it and shouting all sorts of obscenities. I felt violated and used.

Then suddenly, it was quickly off of me and was standing to one side of the bottom of my bunk bed. A light came through the thin gap in the curtains. There were different shades of a golden light which also had very small particles inside it, like dust or small stars which moved around like little bright lights.

This Reptilian creature was about six-feet tall. I could sense it was either proud or happy with itself, maybe both. I tried to sit up as best I could and through my mind, I swore at it again.

The creature walked forward and stepped into the light beam. As it did, the feet and legs vanished into the light. The more the creature moved forward towards the window, the more of it vanished.

After it was gone, I felt relaxed, but I could still feel where I was held around my throat. I felt I was raped by this horrendous monster.

I awoke to a bright sunny day. I could hear my mother downstairs, washing up and doing housework. I laid in my bed and didn't move a muscle. I ran the incident through my mind *again and, yes, I could still feel where I was held around my throat.*

I know this happened. My mind, heart and soul know that this happened. For the life of me, I could not run downstairs to explain to my mother about this. Who would have believed it? How would my parents have handled such a thing? I did not know what to do?

Since that night, my stepfather passed away. I asked my mother if she believed in aliens or UFOs. She replied that my stepfather said once that he saw a UFO near Brighton while at sea in the 1960s and he swore that it was a UFO, but only told my mother this.

I never told my mother about my experience, as I thought it would be too harrowing for her to hear.

What do I do about my experience? I would love to do something about it. It may help somebody, as I am being very honest. Things like this should be disclosed. An answer has to be found on why this is happening." RR

These type of attacks by Reptilian beings are known to occur. The witness stated that the creature seemed to 'feel proud of itself' for its actions. I have heard similar comments from others who have encountered these beings. David Eckhart told me that it was his experience that the Reptilians despised humans, and that they had a habit of belittling abductees; though it was their duty to tolerate humans as much as possible.

I RECEIVED the following account not long after I had posted Gregor's encounter in an Austrian cave:

I received this intriguing typed letter in March 2012 from 'Jerry' (not the witness' real name) who now lives on the US west coast. No contact information was given. A bit of personal information was removed in order for me to preserve the witness' anonymity:

"Sir - this is the first time I am disclosing my experience to the public. My family has been previously informed of the details. At the time, I owned a small business which I had started after I finished a twelve-year stint in the military. I was then living near Eldridge, Missouri and was raised in the general area and knew the terrain fairly well. I had spent time at the US Army Engineer School in Fort Leonard Wood, Missouri and some of the training included spelunking. When I left the Army, I continued to explore caves as recreation.

In 1993 I helped form a local group of experienced 'cavers.' We would get together on weekends and explore some of the cavern systems throughout Missouri and Arkansas. The experience I am about to describe took place in the summer of 1995. I was on my own that day, which was not uncommon.

I had decided to check out a cave in Camden County, Missouri which was part of a fairly large system in the area. From what I could tell, this particular cave had not been explored for a long period of time. The entrance was very narrow and well-hidden. After squeezing through the opening, I descended another fifty feet or so before the cave began to open up into a series of chambers. I moved through several of these chambers taking my time to examine the area for possible artifacts and formations. I finally reached, what I thought, was the end of the cave.

I started to hear a rustling sound that was echoing from a small opening near the top of the chamber. I assumed the sounds were bats and didn't pay much attention to it. But after a while I heard motorized sounds and talking. I stood and listened for several minutes wondering what was on the other

138

side of this chamber. The opening was about 10 feet above me. I maneuvered my way up to the opening which was flat and narrow but big enough for me to get a decent look into it.

As I positioned myself to the front of the opening, I started to see light at the other end. The passageway was only a few feet long, but it was just too narrow for me to move through. As I looked through the opening there was a very warm draft of air hitting my face. As well, the air had an acrid vinegar-like odor. There was a very large and well lit 'room' with limestone walls. I noticed a small vehicle that looked like a golf cart but was very low to the ground and without wheels. I continued to observe until I started to hear voices that were getting louder and nearer. Something was making its way towards the vehicle. I had to rub my eyes because I didn't believe what I was looking at.

This 'creature,' because it was not a man, stood about seven-foot and had brown scaly skin. The face and head were shaped like a human with a flat nose but there were no ears or hair. The top of the head had a slight scaly ray or ridge that extending down the back of the neck. From what I could see it had lips and regular sized eyes. The arms were very long and muscular with human-like hands. It also had a massive five-foot tail that tampered to a point. It was dressed in a gold metallic outfit with long pants and shoes. It also carried an oval pack attached to its back.

I watched as this thing was looking at something on the vehicle. I had a high-speed camera which I use to document my cave explorations. I was able to obtain a few distorted images of the being. For some reason while I was taking photos the creature stopped and turned, looking in my direction. I'm not sure if it heard me but it definitely knew of my presence. It then made a terrible 'hissing' sound as it continued to look in my direction. That was enough for me. I quickly started making a beeline out of the cave. When I reached the entrance, I was shaking and hyperventilating. I finally reached my vehicle and drove home.

I continued to explore caves in the area. I have heard stories of people encountering strange underground beings, but I have never disclosed my experience. A few years after this incident I went back to the cave but was unable to get near it since the area is now government property. I can assume that I witnessed something that I was not supposed to see. It pains me to think what secrets are being kept from us. To those who say that there are no non-humans living among us, well, think again. They are here. I do have the aforementioned evidence of the experience, but I do not wish to release this at the present time." Jerry

The witness indicated that the photographs he obtained were discernible enough to indicate that this was a Reptilian being. I was not able to communicate with the witness after our initial contact. There had been a well-known report of a Reptilian encounter in a cave system near Carthage, Missouri a few years prior to this incident. That encounter was said to have taken place at a US military facility that was used for supply storage.

THE NEXT ACCOUNT was forward to me in April 2013:

"Hello - I would like to tell you about an experience I had in 1954 while working with the US Naval engineers at Zaragoza Air Base near Zaragoza, Spain. This was to be a refurbished NATO facility. I was a contractor (24-years-old and working for my father's construction firm) and hired by the DoD. This

was my first time away from the United States. I had another fellow with me who had worked for my father for a couple of years.

Only a few people knew of my experience; my wife (who is deceased) and two close friends (who have also passed away). I have read some of the stories of other people you have published. I thought that I could add my story to the record.

After I had been in Spain for several weeks, I decided to take in the surroundings. I was told by some of the locals that the Monasterio de Piedra near Nuevalos would be an excellent place to visit. The monastery was about sixty miles away, so I decided it would be an enjoyable day trip. When I arrived, I met a young lady who offered to show me around the complex. It was a very hot day (early August) so we took numerous breaks along the way.

As the afternoon waned and the early evening approached, it was time for me to head back toward Zaragoza. The young lady mentioned that there was a very nice inn not far from the monastery if I wanted to stay the night, then get an early start in the morning. So, I decided to stay the night; maybe do some exploring that evening.

The inn was very rustic, though quite comfortable. I had dinner outside on the back patio. It was an excellent evening. Though it was dusk, I could still see the terrain not far from the inn. There was a vineyard and a small lavender meadow behind the inn which led to a series of rocky outcrops. I thought that I would take a look around, but I first asked the owner if it was fine to do so.

I walked through the vineyard and reached a small pond, which had a loud chorus of frogs. By this time, it was dark, but there was a fair amount of available moonlight, though I still needed a flashlight to see where I was going. I walked around the pond and started to cross a small bridge over a narrow *stream. As I walked over the bridge, I noticed something run through the water about fifty feet up stream. There was enough moonlight to where I could make out an upright shape. This thing was heading toward the high rocks, though I lost sight of it.*

I stood silent for about five minutes. It was eerie because the frogs were now quiet. The only sound was coming from the direction of the rocks and the noise was very strange. It sounded like a guttural 'yak-yak-yak' series, that would pause for a few seconds, then repeat. It would also fade in and out. After a few minutes, it stopped. I had no idea what it was.

I crossed the bridge and started to slowly approach the rocks. As I came to the rock face, there was a fairly well-worn trail on the ground along the edge. I walked further until I reached an opening in the rock face. I pointed the flashlight inside and saw that it was a grotto about fifteen-foot deep and high enough for me to stand in. The floor of the grotto was littered with small animal bones, so I figured there were predators about; most likely fox.

I continued on the trail until I heard the 'yak-yak-yak' sound again and it was very close. I instantly stopped walking and started searching around me with the flashlight. Just then, some gravel landed on me and the loud 'yak-yak-yak' sound was coming from above me.

I quickly looked up and pointed the flashlight. There was a creature standing on a small ledge about 15-foot away, staring at me with yellow eyes reflecting back. It was screaming 'yak-yak-yak' in quick constant rhythm.

This was the ghastliest thing I've ever witnessed. It was standing on two legs and was about four to five foot tall. I've read about Reptilian encounters on your blog. Well, I think this may have been one. It was dark in color and had arms like a human. The face looked like that of a lizard; resembling an iguana.

After a few seconds it leaped off the ledge onto the trail; swiftly running on two legs in the opposite direction. It was then that I noticed a long tail as it moved away from me.

I quickly made my way back toward the inn and directly to my room. I laid in bed thinking about this creature the entire night. I was terrified to look out my window, fearing that it had followed me back to the inn.

Early in the morning I checked out and drove back to Zaragoza. I have no proof to my experience other than my word. But I now believe that this was a Reptilian creature."
HY

I was able to have a conversation with the witness a few days after I received their email. There were no changes to the original account or embellished details. The witness still seemed a bit nervous about his experience, even after all the years had passed.

IN 2010, David Eckhart referred me to an experiencer who I will refer to as 'Matt R.' I eventually received an email from this person:

"I am a former New Orleans Police Department officer, who had several Reptilian abductions in 2005. These involved paramilitary type training scenarios. As a consequence of these abductions, I experienced strange physiological symptoms. I developed new allergies, my senses became overly sensitive, and my body temperature dropped around three to

LON STRICKLER

four degrees. I've been blood tested, and it's not a thyroid condition.

As you may have heard, there have been a series of Reptilian sightings on the west coast of Florida. The two locations are Punta Gorda and North Port, Florida. I traveled to one of these hotspots a few months ago and had a close encounter with a large winged Reptilian.

Around midnight, columns of light descended into the neighbor's yard; like silent lightning. A few hours later, I could hear large creatures rustling in the bushes. At around 2:30 a.m., one of the creatures struck a large tree in half with a single blow. It's important to note that a tree smashing event happened in North Port, a few weeks before my experience. One witness in that area claimed that a Reptilian cracked a fallen tree trunk in half, as the witness jogged by (in order to intimidate the witness).

I deliberately went into the woods with no flashlight, no camera, and no weapon. I knew they were far too smart to approach if I had any of these devices on my person. I didn't manage to get any sort of telepathic communication, but I am the only visitor to the site to get such a violent reaction. The owner of the property, Tom, is able to testify to the fact that I was fifty yards away from that large tree when it was smashed, and there wasn't anyone else in the woods.

At around 4:30 a.m. that night, I loudly announced that I was going back inside the nearby house, and I was done for the evening. I had spent all night pacing along the tree line, in the dark, and was quite upset at the Reptilian's hesitancy to approach. They had no reason not to approach me; I didn't have any weapons, cameras or lights.

Shortly after I entered the back porch, one of the Reptilians let out a loud sigh, that trailed off into an alligator type growl. Clearly, it thought I was done for the night, and had gone all *the way back inside the house. I ran back outside and proceeded to criticize further about its inability to approach me. The sounds it made were identical to the growls heard on the Eckhart tapes, especially the deeper guttural tones (Note: David had recorded many sounds made by the beings in his house).*

It's important to note that the local witness has seen a pair of white albino winged Draco type aliens in the area for many months (as have several neighbors, and his sons). These same Reptilians have recently taken to vandalizing his truck. In one incident, the larger winged Draco punched the side mirror off his truck with such force that it woke all of the dogs in the neighborhood, and sent the mirror flying a great distance. It could not have been a car, because it was parked in a locked, gated driveway. This happened around 3 a.m., just like the tree smashing I witnessed." Matt R

I later verified these incidents with the residents in North Port, Florida. It was my opinion that something very unusual was occurring in the surrounding neighborhood. It's interesting to note that MUFON was made aware of the activity, then suddenly stopped investigating once other residents began submitting similar reports. Some of the physical evidence and photographs were compelling, even though I was never given permission to publish.

The areas in and around Punta Gorda, North Port and Arcadia, Florida have been significant 'hot spots' for anomalous activity for several decades. The Myakka River State Park is also included in this region; a location well-known for Skunk Ape sightings.

Matt R. had talked on several occasions, especially after I received the following email from him:

"My friend's phone has been sending text messages by itself. The messages are sexually explicit. They've been sent to men and women in his contact directory. The grammar seems to have an overly perfect style, but also has a strange tone to it. It is reminiscent of the strange 'antiquated' dialect of English that David Eckhart has heard the Reptilians use. Whoever is writing these, doesn't speak normal domestic USA English.

He is also receiving 'dead air' calls from 11-digit numbers, which should be impossible. There are no 11-digit phone numbers. He is an attorney, and partner at a major law firm in Chicago. He has no interest in UFO subject matter. His only connection is his friendship with me. This started around the beginning of the month (April 2010). It was also during this time period that the North Port and Punta Gorda victims began having strange phone issues. These include phones calling people by themselves, strange numbers, and sudden phone outages. My phone has called other people, by itself, several times. Now, both my younger siblings are being harassed (brother and sister). This makes a total of five people I know who are receiving this type phone harassment. There are mysterious inhuman voices heard within phone calls and more phantom text messages.

My primary objective was still to de-escalate the tension that was occurring. The North Port and Punta Gorda victims were both terrified by these Reptilian sightings. I spent dozens of hours talking them out of shooting at the beings! I go out in the woods, offering to write down whatever statement the Reptilians were willing to make. For some reason, this infuriated the aliens. Apparently, enough to harass everyone I know.

I have to report this activity. If it is a precursor to my disappearance or death, I want it to be on record." Matt R

The following background information from Matt R. includes recollections of his abduction and his assessment of the Reptilians and their agenda:

"I served in the 8th District, New Orleans Police Department, New Orleans, LA. My badge number was 1765. I was one of the few hundred officers that stayed throughout the Katrina disaster.

I had a few Reptilian abductions back in 2005. You may already be familiar with the Reptilian sightings in New Orleans after Katrina. These were documented by Joe Montaldo's group, ICAR. Both Police and National Guardsmen had simultaneous sightings and missing time. Groups of Reptilians were seen 'patrolling' parts of the city eight days after the storm. However, my abduction actually took place a few weeks before Katrina. I was forced to act as an extra in a 'training session' for the warrior-class Reptilians.

I was brought to what was a shopping mall type setting. There's no way for me to be certain if this was an actual mall or some underground training replica. I still vividly remember the ornate decorative lamp posts that lined the main corridor. Although the mall had a roof, it also had expensive cobblestone style flooring. Design wise, it seemed to be a very upscale mall.

There were dozens of other human abductees. Most were dressed as civilians. I was one of the few dressed as police. The police 'uniform' I wore was non-descript; no badges, no markings. We were instructed to stand near an intersection of two major corridors and wait. The lights went out, then there was a large explosion.

The Reptilians either bored, or explosively breached, via a hole in the roof of the mall's center point. Literally, seconds after this blast, the Reptilians were running down this hallway. I don't know if they teleported in or jumped down.

Either way, they hit the ground level too quickly to have used ropes. They were all brown-scaled and about seven to eight foot tall. They immediately began firing weapons over people's heads. They shot the lighted sign fronts and those lamp posts. They even shot a garbage can. This produced a shower of debris and sparks. Three out of the four Reptilians didn't have weapons. The few who did were carrying powerful backpack powered laser-type weapons. The backpacks themselves were extremely thin and barely thicker than a laptop. But everything they shot exploded into flames instantly. I don't know if these weapons were particle beams or infrared. If I had to guess, I'd say some kind of infrared or plasma. The heat between the end of their guns and the targets was visible. The air shimmered like the heat above a large flame. They took specific care to target objects near people so that the shrapnel and noise would cause them to run. Within a few seconds, everyone was fleeing from the advancing troops.

After the herd of panicked people tried to flee for the nearest exit, they were blocked by another wave of a dozen or so Reptilians. The few generic 'police' actors were then made to stand up on a nearby pedestal. It looked to be some kind of abandoned red, plywood style stage. It must have already been cleared of its decorations or was between holiday uses. My fellow 'police' and I handed over our weapons and allowed ourselves to be frisked. We were then allowed to leave.

After this was demonstrated to the crowd, the Reptilians began rapidly frisking them for weapons, contraband and stolen goods. After being frisked, they were told to exit the mall. The Reptilians did all of this instruction in pantomime, with a lot of excited waving and pointing. That's where my recollection ends. I've had no other conscious abductions since. However, I did have a number of permanent nervous system/physiological changes. I don't remember any of the

medical abductions where those modifications took place."
Matt R.

At one point, Matt R. included his thoughts as to why these maneuvers were conducted. He also claimed to have received telepathic insight of their plans. It was obvious to him that the Reptilians had a precognitive sense that Hurricane Katrina was going to occur and that they were aware of the chaos that would follow. Were they working with or supporting the government and military in some capacity?

The Reptilian conspiracy accounts and theories are quite prolific. There have been thousands of articles and books written about it. Matt R. continues to summit his personal investigative findings to me, and I allow his point of view to be presented. Do I find any fact in his assessments? Well, I've heard and seen a lot of unexplained phenomena over the years. I find it prudent to not make assumptions based on personal bias. Many times, you will be proven wrong.

9

DEATH ON MONTOUR RIDGE

THE DISAPPEARANCE and eventual death of 39-year-old Todd Sees has been one of the most mysterious cases in modern ufology.

In the early morning of August 4, 2002, Todd Jeffrey Sees rode his ATV, starting at his home at the base of Montour Ridge in Northumberland County, PA. (Point Township), on a short jaunt up a mountain trail adjacent to a sprawling high-power line. After he failed to return home by noon, the family became concerned and notified the authorities.

A massive search effort ensued, which included search & rescue personnel (with search dogs and helicopters), local & state police, as well as an organized search team that numbered over two hundred volunteers. The entire area from the top of the ridge, adjacent woods and the family property was explored, including a small pond located seventy feet from the Sees house. Divers and dogs searched the area in and around the pond without success.

The entire six square miles of the ridge were searched. The ATV was located one mile from the Sees residence and showed no signs of damage or mechanical issue. The key for the ATV was missing and to-date were never found. No personal effects were found at the location of the ATV.

The District Attorney and County Coroner were on-site along with paramedics. The search concluded as soon as darkness fell and was to continue the next morning at first light. The weather that day was had ninety degree lows with 0.01 inches of rain.

On August 5th at 7:35 pm, Sees body was located under a fallen tree in heavy under growth on his property fifty yards from his home near the trail searchers were using to access the ridge. He had no boots, or coveralls. He was wearing cut-off jeans, a t-shirt and socks. The body showed moderate to severe stages of decomposition.

The County Coroner pronounced Mr. Sees dead at 9:04 pm. The body was removed from the scene and taken to Lehigh Valley Hospital for autopsy, which was scheduled for August 6, 2002 at 11:45 a.m.

The death was ruled as 'fatal cocaine toxicity' despite evidence suggesting that something else most likely occurred. The circumstances involving the recovery, handling, autopsy and final arrangements with the body are also mired in controversy.

A joint investigation by Butch Witkowski / Cold Case Unit of the UFO Research Center of PA and Lon Strickler of the Phantoms & Monsters Fortean Research team has uncovered previously undisclosed information on this incident.

Although several reports have been written on this case by other researchers, none of the summaries paralleled documented facts found by our investigation. There were issues raised almost immediately after reading reports from local news media, UFO reporting agencies and law enforcement. Each contained major discrepancies in some form or another.

A few of these false statements, documented by Butch Witkowski, were as follows:

- One Sees boot found in tree near ATV.
- Timber Rattlesnake found next to body.
- Strange burn mark on forehead.
- Coroner spurious interviews.
- Sees had a long history of drug abuse.
- Sees' body was mutilated.
- Body was removed and taken to Fort Indiantown Gap for an autopsy.
- Three different people claimed to identify the body.
- Local police stated they were handling the case.
- FBI on scene and advised all to maintain secrecy.
- Local police claim to find cocaine in pocket of coveralls retrieved by family.
- Horrific rainstorm 2nd day of search.
- Internet claims of Sees being an undercover DEA agent.

Butch Witkowski also states some of the high strangeness issues of this case:

Sees would have had to walk 1 mile from the ATV location over extremely rocky terrain in socks with an amount of cocaine in his body that would have killed a hardcore drug user in minutes.

During this alleged one mile trek to the area where is body was found on his property, he was never seen by any searchers; even though he would have had to cover a good amount of open land.

The case was kept open by the District Attorney's office for years. This fact has not been proven. Although the local police claimed jurisdiction, the case was handled by the Pennsylvania State Police.

A number of UFO reports did occur during the Sees incident and documented information by two officers on an unrelated call on August 4th near the scene verify previous reports.

Normal public records check showed Sees basically didn't exist.

Interviews with friends and co-workers of Sees and long-time classmates claim Sees was not a drug user. Follow-ups with local and state drug abuse agencies indicate no record of Todd J. Sees.

Per the autopsy report Sees was a healthy 39-year-old male with no physical issues except minor cut and bruises. He was disease free. He showed no signs of prolonged drug use of any kind, either internally or externally.

Due to the ongoing investigation, no further information will be offered on autopsy information and research until the case is closed. The same six original investigators, along with the Phantoms and Monsters Fortean Team, hope to bring this case to a close as soon as possible. It has been 10 years since we started looking into this incident. New information has been slow to materialize.

IN THE MEANTIME, the following questions must be asked:

- Did Todd Sees encounter someone nefarious that day on Montour Ridge?
- Was it a case of an alien abduction gone bad?
- Or was it something else all-together?

— Butch Witkowski

I BECAME interested in the Todd Sees death incident not long after I began to read some of the accounts online. There was scant information available for almost a decade.

In 2013, while attending the Phenomenology Conference in Gettysburg, PA, Sean Forker and I began to discuss the Sees case. I mentioned my frustration at not being able to gather additional evidence on the case, but soon decided that I was going to take up the search once again.

Not long after the conference, I republished an article in the blog referencing the case and asked my reader for possible clues. About a week later, I received a telephone call from Butch Witkowski from UFORCOP. We decided to jump head-first into the case.

Butch had been investigating Sees death for several years, and he had a lot of new and interesting clues. But at that point, it was a matter of going back over all the available evidence and then determine what seemed plausible.

I wanted to go back at look at the area in and around the Montour Ridge. I was beginning to believe that there was a high probability that an actual physical abduction had occurred.

I posted an update on the blog in reference to the Todd J. Sees death investigation and the UFORCOP team's current consensus according to the information and evidence. It has become obvious to the team that Sees' death was the result of unexplained and extraordinary circumstances. The evidence suggests that Sees' body was positioned, then discovered, at a location that had been searched extensively during the time he was missing. In other words, we believe the body was placed at the scene shortly before it was found. That being said, we had not discounted intervention by unknown forces; possibly other-worldly.

During the time of Mr. Sees' disappearance, two subsequent sightings of a saucer-shaped UFO occurred; both reports were forwarded to NUFORC. These reports suggested that a human figure was seen being transported, by means of a beam of light, into the underside of the UFO. The location was above the Montour Ridge along a high-power line. For several decades, this general area has had its share of reports detailing UFO activity.

On September 14, 2002 at 1:45 p.m., approximately three weeks after the Sees incident, a large silver disk-shaped UFO was reported to me by a resident in Northumberland, PA. The UFO was hovering above the Montour Ridge, very near the Sees property. The witness, who was an attorney in the area, stated that they estimated that the craft was over four hundred feet in diameter, fifteen hundred feet above ground and silent. There was a soft glow around the craft which allowed a visual description. It hovered for approximately thirty-seconds, then disappeared completely. I received the report on September 17, 2002, before I had any knowledge of the Sees incident.

The following are a few reports forwarded to the MUFON CMS after the 9/14/2001 sighting:

"Northumberland, PA - 8/2009: It was August 2009 and my father (Age 53 at the time), my brother (21), my boyfriend (29) and myself (24) were house sitting for my boyfriend's sister. Her home is isolated and sits atop a mountain outside Northumberland, PA. It is surrounded by trees which frame an outstandingly clear view of the sky. We were inside the house, chatting and finishing dinner (about 9 or 10 o'clock) when we heard a very strange sound, a low roar that lasted no more than a few seconds, but was quickly followed by what we thought was an earthquake.

The house is huge by anyone's standards, three floors, five bedrooms, five bathrooms, and built solid. It would take quite a natural force to shake the whole thing. The vibration was enough to rattle items on shelves, but it lasted only a second or two. We were startled because the weather was beautiful, no clouds or rain or wind. It was a perfect summer night. We didn't know what to make of it, so we went about our business, clearing dishes and then stepping out onto the upstairs patio to enjoy the night. We hadn't been outside for long when I noticed a strange "star" in the sky. I thought I had seen it move, so I watched it. It began turning different colors; red, green, white, blue, so I quickly pointed it out to the others. They picked it out of the sky right away and the four of us watched as it moved, ever so slightly, as if it were hovering in place. The lights came and went, and almost looked like they were rotating, as if the object they were attached to was spinning. We were all pretty convinced that this was not a star that we were looking at, when it started darting in short spurts. It would hover, then dart to the right, then up, then back to its starting position. It didn't travel far in these spurts, but it was moving in ways that no plane could. We were utterly convinced that this was something none of us had seen before.

We watched, in awe, for about half an hour; all of us staring at the sky, unable to explain what we were seeing, when all of a sudden, it disappeared. Just like that. All the rest of the stars in the sky were visible, it wasn't a cloud. It just... vanished. We all kind of gasped and cursed and got excited when it suddenly reappeared in a completely different region of the sky. We didn't witness it traveling to that spot; but we should have. It was inexplicable. It hovered and darted in that spot for about a minute when all of a sudden it flashed a bright light and began coming toward us!

I know this sounds unreal, and maybe that's why I've kept our story between the four of us and a few close friends for 2 *years, but I swear to you that this next experience has changed all of our lives forever. We cannot explain what we saw. We saw the bright light, and then we saw this giant, black mass coming right at us. I will never know how it traveled from a distance relative to stars to the rooftop so quickly. It was literally seconds. We all kind of screamed, watching the light get closer, but never taking our eyes off of it. It came so close that we thought it would begin to knock over treetops or crash into the house.*

The object we saw was enormous. It dwarfed the house and the property and was the blackest black, with no details visible except for a few orangish white lights on the bottom. It was shaped like a guitar pick and it seemed as if these dull lights were placed in the corners of the triangle. It was traveling fast and made NO SOUND. It is impossible for something so gigantic to fly. It is even more impossible for it to do so silently. As it flew directly over the house, I ran inside, through the house and out a door on the opposite side to catch the rest of its descent. I saw the mass, but it was so low that I lost it to the trees as soon as it passed. We were hysterical. My father and I were yelling, excited and scared at the same time, recounting what we have just seen. My boyfriend was quiet, stunned, not sure how to react. My brother solemnly whispered; "Holy F***, that was the Starship Enterprise," not trying to be funny, but in a reflective, shocked manner.

We all went over the sequence of events a hundred times that night, and probably hundreds since then. We assumed no one outside the house would take us seriously, so we kept it to ourselves. The family and close friends we did tell gave us pitying looks and offered up explanations like 'planes' and 'search lights.' That is not even close to what we saw. We are all level headed, educated people, and we were the first to try and debunk what we were seeing, but we could not. This experience has changed our lives, and I think that we are finally ready for real answers and real input. Was the strange sound/shaking of the house related to what we saw? Why did it come so close to us? Where did it go? Did it land? How could it have been so big? WHAT WAS IT?? It has taken me a year and a half to share my story, but I have thought about this every day. I live not even 2 miles from where this sighting took place and have since witnessed other UFO activity which I would happily share with anyone who is interested or willing to offer answers, but what happened on that night is the most haunting experience of my life. I need to know what we saw." – MUFON CMS "Northumberland, PA - 2/22/2011: Let me begin by saying that I am very reluctant to file this report. I had an experience a year and a half ago which I did not disclose until 6 days ago when I filed my first report with MUFON. I spoke to an investigator on Monday, and then I had this terrifying experience on Tuesday. I have not seen anything since my first sighting in 2009. Now, one day after talking to your investigator, I have been visited up close and personal. I am not saying that one led to the other, but it is a very eerie coincidence. I was out on my deck Tuesday night and I noticed a few "flashing stars," not unlike what I had seen in my first report. It was 9 o'clock. These "stars" were then accompanied by these randomly flashing orbs that were descending to rooftop level. Then I saw a bright red flashing object low to the ground. It was not a plane, and it disappeared after a minute or two. After that, the real chaos began. Around 9:30, I noticed a huge streak of blue/white light flash across the sky, and after that, they were everywhere. Little flashes of what looked like laser beams, but they were coming from all directions and not from one source in the sky. There was a bright hovering orb directly in front of my house, and these little flashes of light were surrounding me. One came within 5 feet of me. They were constant. I was quite scared.

I ran inside and called my brother to let him know what was happening; when I heard a helicopter fly over my house so low that I was almost shouting to make myself heard on the phone. I was on the phone for about 10 minutes, and during that time I counted 3 more helicopters and 2 planes fly directly over my house. They must have been very low for me to hear them from inside my home while on the telephone. After I hung up, I went back out on to the deck. At this time, there were planes and helicopters everywhere, but the bright orb in the sky was still above me (about a block or two away and the height of the planes flying at it) but hovering, not flying. The flashes of light were still all around. Some were in the distance, some were high in the sky, some were on the street, and some were in the alley directly in front of me. I began to feel strange. Not ill, but my stomach began to feel very odd. It was uncomfortable, almost an empty feeling as if I hadn't eaten in days.

By this time I was getting really worried, and the helicopters kept coming. The flashing beam phenomenon was practically happening on my deck, so I quickly came back inside out of fear. I called around and found that some of my neighbors were also aware of the heavy air traffic. One had actually heard all the commotion while in the shower and had gotten dressed and gone outside to see if there was an air raid or something. None had witnessed the lasers or orbs, but these were so low and directly in front of my house... so unless you were in my backyard, they would have been obstructed by other houses and trees. The 10-20 planes in the sky at any given time were visible to everyone though. I am sure that others had to have seen what I witnessed last night. I watched all of this go on for about an hour total. I was home alone, so I was very disturbed, especially since the lights were coming so close to me.

I came back inside and continued to hear planes and helicopters go by one after another until about 11:30. Around that time, I went back outside and saw that the bright orb was moving away from my house toward the farms and fields beyond. I watched it move slowly away, still flashing beams of light in the distance. The planes were still flying by. I went back out at 12:30 and the orb was gone. In its place there were two sets of three lights in the shape of triangles, with planes flying at them. By this time, my mind was exhausted, and I just couldn't comprehend anything else, so I came inside and tried to go to bed.

On Wednesday morning I found out that my father had also seen strange orbs in the woods by the creek on his property earlier that night, around 8 o'clock. He said they looked like lanterns but were sporadic and would disappear after a few seconds. I am not sure that they are related, but he lives about 25 minutes from me, and it is very odd that we both saw similar phenomenon on the same night after almost 2 years of not seeing anything else substantial. I am at a loss for words when it comes to describing just how unreal and amazing last night's events were. There must be someone else out there that witnessed that same thing. It left Northumberland PA and headed toward Danville PA around 11:30-12. Anyone driving Route 11 at that time must have noticed an unusual number of low flying planes if not the orb and flashes themselves." - MUFON CMS

There have been thirty UFO-related sighting reports to MUFON for Northumberland County, PA since 1995.

Since our initial report in February 2013, some of Todd Sees' personal information has come to light. But more data and intelligence will be needed in order to form a reasonable hypothesis for this incident.

Some of the documented facts and evidence-based deductions include:

- There was a cover-up by local officials and, most likely, Federal officials.
- There were reports that the FBI was involved. It seems more likely that this was a military operation (USAF) and that all people involved with the search, including the family, were instructed not to disclose any information.
- Todd Sees body was found in an area, on his property, that was searched by officials and trained dogs. It seems reasonable to assume that the body was placed at the recovery area.
- The physical condition of the body was inconsistent with the amount of exposure and time of death recorded.
- The toxicology report and the coroner's determination of death was inconsistent with the time and evidence provided.
- Much of Todd Sees personal information was unavailable after his death, though some information was made available immediately after our on-air disclosure in February 2014.
- There are many other inconsistencies and false data that were found and/or being investigated. Some of the newer intelligence is currently being researched by our groups.
- Since September 2013, there have been other groups who have stated that they are now looking into the Sees case; after sitting on their collective

hands for over a decade. Much of bluster was created after Butch and I made our assessment in February 2014. Since then, we have been subjected to countless attacks by others; namely, a few individuals associated with Pennsylvania MUFON. The fact is, we uncovered startling details that others now want to take credit for. As well, there is a concerted effort to maintain the cover-up associated with the death of Todd Sees.

- Though the investigation has not concluded, the team has begun to formulate a probable scenario as to what occurred and why Todd J. Sees died. The only statement we could give at this time is that, as of 1/22/2016, the UFO abduction theory has a greater than fifty percent likelihood to have transpired as an aspect to this case. This information is in accordance with the evidence we currently have.

- Hopefully, further evidence will surface in the future. If and when we have a more concrete theory as to what happened to Todd J. Sees, we will surely offer our finding to the public.

10

A HIGHER INTELLIGENCE

IN THE SPRING OF 2017, Paul J. Lucas related a personal close encounter to me and my associate Butch Witkowski. I later asked Paul to transcribe the account, which he gladly produced and forwarded:

"On August 2, 2014 I had a close encounter. I was not taken (abducted, that I can remember) nor did I see any entity but was simply 'shown' a very large strange craft. My experience was as follows and this is what I remember very clearly and distinctively.

We were at a friend's fishing 'camp' north of President, PA, on the upper Allegheny River. This is a very remote area. There were twelve of us standing around a huge bonfire drinking and talking at approximately 10:30 p.m. at night. I wasn't drinking heavily since I had a six-hour drive the next morning back home to northern Virginia after being at the camp for a week with buddies. We've been going up to this camp since our time high school.

Simply stated, it was like time had stopped. Through the smoke of the huge bonfire I could see a craft hovering above, very close to the group, no more than twenty yards away; maybe closer, and it was blinking a light at me. I say, "Me?", because I could feel or sense that it was communicating to me directly. It was like I was in a trance and when I looked away it seemed I was in very slow motion and then looked back and it was there doing it again (blinking a light at me). My friends were motionless. It was like they were frozen in time, but I could see the fire burning and the smoke from the fire curling upwards. But it was like everyone else was, including myself, frozen. There was no psychic message received or remembered per say, but it was like I was simply shown the craft until it was gone. Total time of the incident was maybe two minutes.

Immediately after the event I knew it had happened and looked around as everything was back to normal. Everyone was still around the bonfire talking, drinking, laughing etc. I didn't say anything to anyone. It seemed like my memory of this encounter was delayed or blocked, although I knew it happened. I stayed silent about it until I woke up the next morning. After I awoke, I got ready to drive six hours back home. During that drive, I had all these 'questions' and my memory was now perfectly clear of what happened.

Ever since that encounter I think of and envision the incident every single day. It's as if it was tattooed into my memory. So explicit and exact; like it happened just minutes ago. This memory is as strong as the memory of my parent's deaths or the birth of my child. I can visualize the craft perfectly, but I cannot draw it and have tried many times. It was a design I have never seen before. I looked at many hundreds of UFO drawings online. The craft I saw was multi-sided and very irregular, between an Octahedron and an Icosahedron shaped object. It was opaque in color, simply flashing a white rectangular light at me that was tilted at an *angle left to right. It was not like any UFO drawing on the internet. It doesn't haunt me, though I have many questions.*

I have talked to two respected scientists through my connections here in Washington, DC and both of them said that they have heard of hundreds of similar experiences and that communication might have taken place on a subconscious level. They also stated that I should feel excited or special that I was chosen to receive contact.

I was told by one scientist that 'they' were more than likely one of the 'Grey' species that visit us. These species are good, sort of 'watchers' and selectively contact people on the subconscious level. He went on to say that we don't know or understand what they want, or what they derive from these contacts, but it has been going on as far back as our history takes us.

I have read many books that the two scientists told me to read and these have just added more questions and curiosity. Here are two of the recommended titles:

'The Holographic Universe' by Michael Talbot

'The Omega Project' by Kenneth Ring, Ph.D.

I have read about three dozen books on UFO's since my experience." Paul J. Lucas

Paul's account is an excellent example of how profoundly an experiencer is affected by a non-physical close encounter.

It's not unusual for contactees to seek answers, and to research other experiencer accounts. The most common questions are; "What do they want?" and "Why me?" Unfortunately, we still don't have many solid explanations.

I RECEIVED the following information in February 2017 from my colleague Jamie Brian:

"The incident we had was on Lake Powell, which straddles Arizona and Utah. We had missing time and our watches were in sync. My husband and I had taken a boat trip there. In the evening, around 8:30 pm or so, we were situated on the shore. It was our last night.

Every night at around 12:30 am, I had been waking up absolutely terrified. On the last three nights of our trip, I saw this UFO up over the mountain area. I believe that it's all Indian land, on a reservation.

I was awakened again on the last night, but this time it looked like it was 5:00 in the morning and we were supposed to be leaving to get the boat back at 4:00 am. I thought that we were late. Anyway, I was in the back of the boat which was in the water. Suddenly I saw this thing ascend out of the water. It was like a platform and I'm thinking; "Am I really seeing this? Are my eyes playing tricks?"

It raised out of the water and it was edged on either side. It's difficult to describe. It was about eight or nine foot across, and it had edges that went down on an angle into the water. It was weird looking. I just saw it raise out of the water, I'm guessing about two feet or three feet. I called out to my husband who was on the front of the boat, "Look at this! Look at this!" And each time he would say; "I'm busy. We got to get going because we're late." But we really weren't late. The time was really 12:30 a.m. The light from this thing in the water illuminated everything around us. Also, the radio wasn't working the entire time we were on the lake." Name Withheld

LAKE POWELL HAS a history of UFO related experiences since the lake was built and filled in 1980. USOs (unidentified submerged objects) have been reported on several occasions. A local UFO investigator made the following statement in November 2010:

> "Many people believe that aliens are just flying around in the sky. But they're not. They are also in the water and on the ground; all around us. What makes this unusual is that the aliens are setting up a base in Lake Powell, a man-made reservoir. This has some of us in the community alarmed.
>
> The National Guard have occasionally been dispatched to keep an eye on things. Something's going on, we just don't know what it is yet"

Authorities had multiple reports from citizens visiting Lake Powell on November 8, 2010. They reported an unidentified object dive into the reservoir. Government authorities were called in to investigate, but they have remained silent. However, many locals know exactly what it is. One local resident commented:

> "It's a UFO. I'm positive of it. We've talked to a number of people around here and they said they've been seeing the object come in and out of the water for the last three months."

I RECEIVED this next account in March 2017:

> "In 1989 while my husband was stationed at Yokota AFB, in Fussa, Japan, outside of Tokyo, we had quite an experience. One night while my husband, myself and three sons were

sleeping, there was a loud knock on the bedroom door. It knocked three times at 3:00 a.m. I got up to see if it was one of the kids, but they were all asleep.

A week later the same thing happened again at 3:00 a.m. The knocking was much harder this time. My husband got up to check but I knew it was not a human. I would not let him answer the door.

Shortly after this we got orders to Wright-Patterson AFB in Ohio. We found a home to buy so we moved in while waiting for all our things to come from Japan, which took a month. We all were in sleeping bags. The boys each had their own bedroom and shared a bath, while our bedroom and bath were on the other side of the house. The first night we were there, at 3:00 a.m., the knocking started by banging on our bedroom door. I was quite upset and asked my husband why did it follow us all this way and what does it want?

At this point I will tell you that since I was a small child, (I am now 67-years-old) I have seen many things that were out of the ordinary. I've also heard many things and had experiences that are unexplained. I have been told that I have the ability to see things and know things. I think it is from some people in my family who have physic abilities.

We heard no more knocking after the first night, but when we went under the house, (it had a very large crawlspace) we found a sawhorse that had a bible opened up to a verse. I cannot remember what it was, but it had a red ribbon laying across it. We left it there since I felt it was to remove something bad.

Our belongings came and we got settled in. My oldest son's friend from Japan came to stay with us for a year since his parents were being transferred to Texas and he did not want to go there right away.

We all started feeling a little odd at times in the house.

One night the boys and I were watching television and cable box started spinning the channel finder and switching from side A to side B. It finally stopped and I put back on the show we were watching. It scared everyone.

A couple of nights later the knocking started up again. First on my bedroom door, then the next night it knocked on two of the boys' doors. The next night it went wild and knocked on all bedroom doors lightly, then pounding harder and harder on each door over and over, until it finally stopped.

A couple of nights passed, and it started again, over and over, so hard that you could see the doors shake. This went on and on night after night for several months, then suddenly stopped. We then noticed that the dining room floor seemed to be spinning or swirling very lightly but we seemed to be able to feel it if standing still. If company came and sat at the dining room table, they would say they felt sick or they left soon after.

A few months later, we heard a knock on the front door, and I froze. I felt that we were in serious danger. My oldest son, who was 18 at this time, and I both answered the door. There were three young men, late twenties or early thirties, who looked like they were poured from the same mold. All were identical, blond hair, sunglasses, dark suites, tan trench coats, same black shoes. All three were the same height and had identical hair styles and cuts. One of them said; "We would like to talk to you. Can we come in?" I said; "No I am cooking dinner right now. What do you want to talk to us about?" he said;

"We are from LDS and are spreading the word." He talked in a deep monotone voice. It was like we were in the 'Matrix' movie. They told us that they were going to each house in the neighborhood. After they left, we went behind a bush to watch where they went. They walked three blocks up the street and *got into a big black car. I believe it was a Lincoln town car. A man was driving wearing a dark coat and black hat like a fedora. They drove off.*

We now were feeling other things in the house like the thermostat would click off and on. We felt it was synced with the base's jet engine repair area called 'Area B.' When the engines were on and being tested the thermostat would turn off and on in sync with engine sounds.

I will say Wright-Patterson AFB has some weird things there. My husband worked in the former Project Blue Book building; the 'Foreign Technology Division.' Top secret place. It is where all the alien stuff went on and I believe still does. 'Hangar 18' is real if you have ever heard of it.

I will say that all we went through, it did get my husband. I found him in a catatonic state on the dining room floor and the doctors could never find anything wrong with all the testing. It's now 2017 and he has never been the same since that day. Everything I have written is 100% true." Paula M

This account had a bit of everything, including the possibility of the 'Men in Black.' I've heard several stories of weird activity in and around Wright-Patterson AFB, but I'm not quite convinced that it's all alien related. This account may have been a poltergeist or a serious haunting. But, then again, it does seem to be a bit more than that.

I BELIEVE that the following account offers some insight as to what many experiencers are already aware of when it comes to a higher intelligence and a possible personal connection with alien beings:

"In the summer of 1965, I was living in the small town of Kermit, Texas. It was just my mother and I, because my father died before I was born; at least that's what my mom said. I never did see any proof of his death or a grave site. I was 10 years old that summer. One evening my friend and I were in her back yard, laying on our backs and looking at the stars. We were talking 'small talk,' when all of a sudden, I got the urge to look towards the western sky. It was like a voice told me to look for a bright light in the west. As I started to look, I saw a bright yellow light getting bigger and bigger. This light was headed towards the ground. I asked my friend if she was seeing this, but she didn't answer. I looked over and she was totally knocked out. I shook her, but she was not responding.

I was worried about her, but then I heard a voice. A man's voice. I turned my head and there was a man standing about twenty feet away. He was tall, I'd say about six and a half foot tall. Once again, he said; "Are you Elsie?" I looked at his face, and it seemed very familiar. The yellow light was stationary in the sky and had dimmed. The man looked at me and smiled. I responded; "Yes, I'm Elsie. Who are you?" He answered; "I believe you know who I am." Then the face became recognizable. He looked like the picture of my father that my mom had on her dresser. "Are you my father?" He shook his head in the affirmative and said; "Yes Elsie, I am."

I sat there on the grass staring at this man. How could he be my father? Where did he come from? He crouched down to his knees. That's when I noticed he was wearing a silver body suit and was barefoot. He looked at me and said, "I have been watching you all your life. I thought it was about time that I introduced myself to you." I started to cry. I really did want to believe that this was my father. I asked; "Didn't you die?" He looked away for a second or two, then looked back at me.

"Elsie, I have a secret. I had to return home before you were born. I had no choice. But I assure you, I did not die."

By this time, I was absolutely confused and upset. I managed to ask him; *"But can you stay here with us now?"* He stood up and said, *"No, I must leave soon. I will see you again when I'm able. I love you Elsie."* I got to my feet and moved towards him. *"Wait, wait; where are you going?"* By that time, he had vanished, and the yellow light ascended at high speed into the stars. I looked into the sky, hoping the yellow light would reappear. I could hear my friend say; *"What's going on?"* I said nothing, turned and walked home.

I never told my mom what happened because I believe it would have upset her. She loved my father deeply and mentioned him often. But she still never told me what happened to him; even when I asked. In July of this year my mom passed away. I recently started going through her private papers and found an envelope with; *"Elsie - Please Read"* written on the front. There was a letter that was dated July 21, 1965, which was the same day on which my mom passed away.

The letter read:

Sweet Elsie,

I know your daddy came to visit you a few days ago. He told me he would. I love your daddy and miss him terribly but he cannot live with us. All I can tell you is that he will come for you one day. On that day we will all be together in a place I have been before. It is another world; another existence that people on Earth would never understand. It is beautiful and wonderful.

I don't know when you'll receive this letter, but if you have your own family by then, they will join us at their time of *departure as well. Stay strong and hopeful. I love you with all of my heart.*

Mom

My husband and I talked about the contents of the letter, and we discussed it with our adult children. We are convinced that our ancestors are extraterrestrials. I know this seems impossible, but I believe that you and others can understand why I feel this way. That is why I am writing you.

My father has not returned in fifty-one years, but my family and I believe that we will ascend to the stars when our day comes." Elsie

I had to read the email three times before I decided to contact Elsie (Not her real name, according to her). We talked on Skype for almost two hours; in fact, I talked to most of the family. They are convinced that they are 'star people' and will join their non-human race when their human bodies die.

I asked if any of them had extra abilities. Elsie and her daughter say that they have very keen intuitions which has become very useful on occasion. Elsie's husband confirmed this; saying that their abilities were 'scary' at times. I asked her husband if he believes he will join the family since he is not a descendant. He said he can only hope but believes he will. Elsie asked that I post the email so others will feel has hopeful as her and her family.

This was one of the more unusual accounts I have ever received; but it was also very uplifting having the opportunity to talk with Elsie and her family. I gained some assurance that many of us on this planet will rejoin our cosmic family's some-day.

I believe that there are many incarnated extraterrestrials and angels on Earth. These 'star people' have many characteristics similar to other humans but express themselves in a way that distinguishes from other individuals. This is a subject I would like to write about and detail one day.

———

I RECEIVED the following witness account in April 2013:

> "This encounter occurred in 1971, while aboard the aircraft carrier, USS John F. Kennedy CVA-67 (now CV-67) in the Bermuda Triangle. I was assigned to the communications department of the Kennedy and had been in this section about a year. The ship was returning to Norfolk, VA after completing a two-week operational readiness exercise (ORE) in the Caribbean. We were to stand down for thirty days, after arriving in Norfolk, Virginia, to allow the crew to take leave and visit family before deploying to the Mediterranean for six months.
>
> I was on duty in the communications center. My task was to monitor eight teletypes printing the 'Fleet Broadcasts.' On the top row were four teletypes each printing messages from four different channels. On the bottom row were four more doing the exact same thing except the signal was carried on different frequencies. If one of the primary receivers started taking 'hits' I would be able to retrieve the message from the bottom one. I also notified Facilities Control of any hits so they could tune the receivers. On the other side of the compartment (room) was the NAVCOMMOPNET (Naval Communications Operations Network). This was the Ship to Shore circuit with the top teletype being the receive and the bottom as the send (known as a duplex circuit). Next to this was the Task Group Circuit for ship to ship communications (task group operations or TGO).

It was in the evening, about 20:30 (8:30 p.m.) and the ship had just completed an eighteen hour 'Flight Ops.' I had just taken a message off one of the broadcasts and turned around to file it on a clip board. When I turned back to the teletypes the primaries were typing garbage. I looked down to the alternates which were doing the same. I walked a few feet to the intercom between us and the Facilities Control. I called them and informed them of the broadcasts being out. A voice replied that all communications were out. I then turned and looked in the direction of the NAVCOMMOPNET and saw that the operator was having a problem. I then heard the Task Group operator tell the watch officer that his circuit was out also. In the far corner of the compartment was the pneumatic tubes going to the Signal Bridge (where the flashing light and signal flag messages are sent/received). There is an intercom there to communicate with the Signal Bridge and over this intercom we heard someone yelling; "There is something hovering over the ship!" A moment later we heard another voice yelling. "It is God! It is the end of the world!"

We all looked at each other. There were six of us in the Comm Center, and someone said; "Let's go have a look!" The Comm Center is amidships, just under the flight deck, almost in the center of the ship. We went out the door, through Facilities Control and out that door, down the passageway (corridor) about 55 feet to the hatch that goes out to the catwalk on the edge of the flight deck (opposite from the 'Island' or that part of the ship where the bridge is). If you have ever been to sea, there is a time called the time of no horizon. This happens in the morning and evening just as the sun comes up or goes down over the horizon.

During this time, you cannot tell where the sea and sky meet. This is the time of evening it was. As we looked up, we saw a large, glowing sphere. Well, it seemed large, however, there was no point of reference. That is to say, if the sphere were low; say 100 feet above the ship, then it would have been about two to three hundred feet in diameter. If it were, say, 500 feet about the ship then it would have been larger. It made no sound that I could hear. The light coming from it wasn't too bright, about half of what the sun would be. It pulsated a little and was yellow to orange.

We didn't get to looked at it for more than about 20 seconds because General Quarters (Battle Stations) was sounding and the Communication Officer was in the passageway telling us to get back into the Comm Center. We returned and stayed there. We didn't have much to do because all the communication was still out. After about twenty minutes, the teletypes started printing correctly again. We stayed at General Quarters for about another hour, then secured. I didn't see or hear of any messages going out about the incident.

Over the next few hours, I talked to a good friend that was in CIC (Combat Information Center) who was a radar operator. He told me that all the radar screens were just glowing during the time of the incident. I also talked to a guy I knew that worked on the Navigational Bridge. He told me that none of the compasses were working and that the medics had to sedate a boatswain's mate that was a lookout on the signal bridge. I figured this was the one yelling it was God. It was ironic that of the five thousand men on a carrier, that only a handful actually saw this phenomenon. This was due to the fact that Flight Ops had just been completed a short time before this all started, and all the flight deck personnel were below resting. It should be noted that there are very few places where you can go to be out in the open air aboard a carrier. From what I could learn, virtually all electronic components stopped functioning during the twenty minutes or so that *whatever it was hovered over the ship. The two Ready CAPs (Combat Air Patrol), which were two F-4 Phantoms that are always ready to be launched, would not start.*

I heard from the scuttlebutt that three or four 'men in trench coats' had landed and were interviewing the personnel that had seen this phenomenon. I was never interviewed, maybe because no one knew that I had seen it.

A few days later, as we were approaching Norfolk, the Commanding and Executive Officers came on the closed-circuit TV system that we had. They did this regularly to address the crew and pass on information. During this particular session the Captain told us how well we did on the ORE and about our upcoming deployment to the Mediterranean. At the very end of his spiel, he said; "I would like to remind the crew, that certain events that take place aboard a Naval Combatant Ship, are classified and are not to be discussed with anyone without a need to know." This was all the official word I ever received or heard of the incident.

Being young and excited about my visit home and going to the Med, I completely forgot about it until years later when my wife and I went to see Close Encounters of the Third Kind at the movies when it first came out. In fact, the friend that had been the radar operator was with his wife and went with us. As we walked across the parking lot to my car, I ask him if he remembered what we had experienced years earlier on the ship. He looked at me and said he never wanted to talk about it again. As he said it, he turned a little pale. I never talked about the incident again. When I discovered; "Aliens and Strange Phenomenon" on MSN and started reading the posts I started thinking about it again. Now I seem obsessed in finding out all I can about this phenomenon." JK

I find military encounters quite fascinating because there is usually a strange caveat included. In this instance, the four 'men in trench coats' incident. Were these Naval officials debriefing personnel, or something a bit more sinister?

THE NEXT ACCOUNT concerns a USO incident near Key West, Florida:

"It was the summer of 2000 and I was just a non-rate stationed on a one hundred and ten foot Coast Guard cutter out of Key West, FL. We had enjoyed three days of calm weather and the seas where glassy smooth. Rare nights like this are when smugglers like to make a run and we were sitting on a darkened ship on a known drug route; an awesome fishing spot due to a massive drop off underneath us. We had our radars set to max, our ears wide open and our mouths clamped shut. Sound carries like crazy out there and sometimes you can hear the engines of a 'go- fast' screaming before radar even picks them up. But this night was dead, no activity at all. I was coming onto the bridge for the 03:30 hours watch shift. Our J.O.D. was checking the equipment for a pass-down but when he got to the radar, he gave a little "WTF" under his breath. The oncoming O.O.D. came over to see what was up, said the same thing then called our C.O. on the sound powered phone. We heard him say; "Hey Cap, we have two contacts moving fast, coming straight at us about forty knots out." So, we think we are about to see some action, and everyone starts getting amped up when we hear him give the speed. "Four hundred knots and holding steady." At this point we think it's just a radar anomaly or some 'running rabbits' radar type echo. But these two staggered contacts stayed on the scope, and their signal just got stronger. Whatever it was, it was the size of a

cargo ship moving about four hundred and fifty miles per hour and wasn't even leaving a wake. (You can see a wake on radar especially on a calm night.) After hearing this the C.O. is on deck in his bathrobe about thirty seconds later just staring at the radar and everyone is just perplexed trying to get a look in over his shoulder. He sends us all out onto the bridge wing with night vision goggles and has us all looking out for these things. Every few seconds he is counting down the range and right when they get to eight miles out, they simply drop off the radar. Boom. Just gone.

Now both of us non-rates get sent down to the bow of the ship and told to listen for anything. So, we listen and it's so quiet that all we can hear is the blood pounding in our ears. Then after not even a minute of vigilance we see something. Two lights underwater moving fast and coming directly at us. If we had blinked, we would have missed them. In just a moment they had past directly under our bow and were gone. The best description I can give would be like two train lights moving slightly staggered, not too deep under crystal clear water. Maybe forty or fifty feet down. The leading vessel was slightly silhouetted by the trailing vessel and the brief impression I got of it was like the engine car of a train, just way larger. It was over so fast I really never got a look so I can't say much more than that about them. My fellow lookout and I exchanged a shocked look at each other, and he asked me if I had just seen it too. We talked excitedly about it for a second and ran back up to report our findings.

After we made it to the bridge and started telling the C.O. what we had seen the Quarter Master shut us up saying they had popped back up on radar. Sure enough, eight miles out, there was the same signal, still moving staggered at four hundred knots. We watched them disappear off radar at about forty plus miles in silence. All of us were just holding our *positions until they passed out of range. Then the old man asked us what we saw. We told him and after a minute of silence he just said. "Weird. Radar glitch it is." Then sighed and went back to bed. After he wished us a good watch and went below deck the C.O.B. (Most senior Chief of the Boat) pulled us up to the flying bridge for a talk. He basically told us that there are lots of weird things out here and that this is not the first time he had heard about 'underwater oddities' from sailors, but it was the first he had ever been a part of. He didn't say we shouldn't tell anyone, but he made it pretty clear most people wouldn't believe us if we did. That was it.*

The next night was just as calm and we ended up stopping a drug smuggler with nearly a ton of product on board. We had all just sort of put the earlier incident behind us and moved on with our normal lives. All I can say after two decades of experience in the military is that in the middle of the ocean on a clear night and with a good set of NVGs you can see little zippy things in the sky, just about every night if you have some patience. In my years of sea-time I've seen lots of odd things, but that night will always stand out in my memories." RO That's a very intriguing account. I have heard of a many strange 'underwater' incidents at sea, especially in the Gulf of Mexico, the Florida Keys and north into the Bermuda Triangle. David Eckhart has maintained that he believes that the underwater facility where he was taken to was in the Gulf of Mexico just off the Florida coast. There have also been continued rumors of USO sightings in the waters near Puerto Rico, in the Biminis and the Bahama Islands."

IN THE SUMMER OF 2019, I received a telephone call from an experiencer (I'll refer to him as 'MT') who is a medical professional living in Palm Springs, CA. As I was listening to the account, it reminded me of the film Close Encounters of the Third Kind because of some similarities. I do believe that MT is sincere, but very 'excitable,' if not for a better word to describe his demeanor. He explained that since this incident, he has experienced other bizarre encounters with unknown entities. His brother and friends have also suffered strange and unexplained events.

This specific incident occurred in the winter of 1999 when MT, his brother and two other friends were young men living in southeast Los Angeles. One afternoon, they were hanging out at one of their homes, when they each experienced an unknown sensation of urgency. As they started to regain their senses, each man described a similar feeling and perception; they must go to a location ASAP! Neither man was specific as to the location, but they somehow knew where to go.

Their urge to get to the mysterious location was so intense that they actually stole a relative's van.

The group climbed into the van and started to drive northeast towards the San Bernardino Mountains, an area that none of the young men was familiar with. As they continued on their trek, they each confirmed to each other that they were heading in the right direction. MT stated that he had no recollection of the trip, other than they were on the correct course. It was starting to get dark, but they were determined to achieve their objective. As they got very near to the location, the entire group screamed in unison; "STOP!" The van was parked on the side of a gravel road, as they quickly piled out of the vehicle. By this time, it was totally dark, but they all knew in what direction they were to walk. They had one flashlight between them.

MT said that they were walking through an area with heavy under brush and large pine trees. It was much cooler than the city, but no one was complaining. He believes that they hiked for about forty-five minutes, until they all knew that they had reached their objective. In a small clearing, a perfectly squared black rock was found. MT thinks it was about five foot square and that each one of them "could see it without the flashlight." He doesn't know how, but that it was 'revealed' to them. They scampered onto the top of the monolith and collapse into a deep sleep.

Then suddenly, they all woke to the sound of something heading in their direction. There were literally hundreds of white orbs in various sizes darting through the trees and canopy. The sounds were unrecognizable, but each of them was scared of what was happening. They immediately jumped off the rock and began to run in the direction of van. The orbs chased them through the forest, buzzing all around the frightened men. They knew that they were getting close to the van, when unexpectedly the orbs disappeared. Within seconds, they were abruptly confronted by several large dark-colored vehicles with bright searchlights. MT said that he doesn't know how or why the vehicles suddenly appeared, but it was like they had manifested from a huge unseen portal or had descended from above.

A loud human voice howled out; "What the hell are you doing here?" MT said that none of them responded to the voice. They were confused as to why they were there and so scared that they were unable to answer. All of a sudden, they were hit with a horrendous bellowing that seemed to come from above, as they all fell to the ground. That is the last thing that either of the young men remembers from the location.

Many hours later, MT said that his brother was shaking him awake. The four men were all in the back of the van, each in anguish from throbbing headaches. MT said he opened the side door; and as the sunlight hit him in face, it literally caused him to become ill. They looked around and realized that they were in a grocery store parking lot. They watched people going about their business, giving them strange glances. MT stated that they eventually figured out that they were in Riverside, CA, but that they had no idea how they got there.

Each of these men have no idea what occurred that day, but they all have experienced strange activity since then. MT says that he and his brother have both had encounters with unknown beings but are not able to recall many details. I asked why he was coming forward after eighteen years. MT said that he wants answers but has been unable to get any information. He doesn't remember the location of the monolith; almost as if it was wiped from his memory. But he and the others know it happened exactly the way it was described.

11

MIB – ARE THEY ALIEN BEINGS?

I'VE BEEN GATHERING and receiving alien experiencer accounts for almost forty years, and the variety of entities and humanoids that people observe continues to expand. In some cases, it's difficult to determine if these entities are actually alien or non-terrestrial beings. For example; the winged humanoid phenomena that my team and I have been investigating for the past few years. At this point, we really have no idea what these beings are. We do believe that they are corporeal but doubt that they are indigenous to this Earth plane. Because of the indecision, I'm not going to classify them as alien beings. At least, not for now.

Another well-known group of unexplained entities are the BEK, or black-eyed kids and adults. Once again, we have very little information available to determine if they are alien beings or a type of hybrid. There is no doubt that they live among us and that they do possess a variety of strange characteristics. But there is just not enough evidence, in my opinion, to say that they are non-terrestrial.

But there has been a group of entities that are part of Ufology lore and are associated with people who experience close encounters. These are the 'men in black' or MIB. These entities usually show up, unannounced, at an experiencer's home seeking information about an encounter with a UFO or extraterrestrial. The presence of these MIB became widely known during the reported UFO activity (and the Mothman encounters) in the Point Pleasant, West Virginia area in the mid to late 1960s. The journalist and Ufologist John A. Keel began writing about the MIB after they made themselves known to the local residents. The descriptions of these MIB were somewhat consistent; pale or olive colored skin, monotone voice, no emotion or expression, dressed in a black suit and fedora, and driving a large black sedan. There were usually two MIB traveling together. But the most disconcerting aspect of their presence occurred after they would conduct a brief interview. They would warn the witness, in no uncertain terms, not to discuss or report what they had encountered. The message was clear. Keep your mouth shut.

Most experiencers and investigators don't know what to make of the MIB. Are they quasi-government agents? How do they know who to contact? In most instances, they appear not long after an encounter and before a report is ever made. They truly are an enigma. The following account was reported in Vancouver, British Columbia, Canada in December 2000. The synopsis of the event was later forwarded to me by a local investigator:

Several days after witnessing two low flying objects over the area, on two separate nights (one of the objects was described as huge, making a rumbling like noise; it had a V-shaped tail with two rows of round and oblong windows and was black, gray, and silver in color) and after receiving a suspicious phone call from someone claiming to be a General from the Canadian armed forces, two strange men appeared at the door of the witness' residence. They produced wallets, one black, one brown, containing photo ID that stated they were from the Canadian Air Defense. They asked to come inside. The witness extended his hand but was ignored.

Moving into the house took them through the kitchen area, but they stopped upon seeing the microwave. After some questioning, the witness lowered a portion of a counter and they carefully slid through the extra space. Sitting down they produced a small silver colored tape recorder and inserted a small disc, between a nickel and a quarter in size. On entering the house one of the men had noticed an unusual walking stick in the hallway, to which he remarked that the head of the stick's carving, painted red, reminded him of primates back home.

The two men were olive skinned and appeared to have slanted eyes. Each wore glasses with thick rims. They wore black suits with black shirts, one had a white tie, and the other was buttoned up to the neck. The one with the tie had a clip that contained a red 'stone' that flickered. The other had a ruby ring surrounded with diamonds. His watch was square but without apparent hands, instead being encircled with buttons that periodically illuminated from white to green to mauve. The strap appeared to be molded into the skin and was a solid steel band. The belt on his pants was of metallic strips with a square buckle. Both had very large feet, estimated to be fourteen inches. Each carried a briefcase that was heavy and cold.

When sitting down they never relaxed into their chairs but retained a stiff back the whole time. Not once during their stay in the house, did they speak to each other. The witness' two cats were extremely agitated the whole time during the visitors stay. Also, the owner's dog that lived upstairs barked during the whole episode.

The men noticed that the witness was wearing a very

unusual watch and one of them touched his arm. The touch felt very cold and clammy. They questioned the witness about his sightings, and one of them appeared to be taking shorthand notes. When they questioned him, they looked into his eyes and seemed to 'pierce his brain.'

As they were leaving, they again carefully avoided the microwave. Outside in the yard they spent about thirty minutes scouring the ground with a Geiger counter. As they rounded the corner of the house the witness went from the kitchen to the bedroom, which gave him a clearer view of the driveway and the road. Despite the very short period of time it took him to achieve this, the two men were not in sight, nor was a car leaving, or no car door could be heard slamming. They had vanished. Later the witness discovered that on the windowsill, only six inches behind where one of the men had been sitting, was a Windex bottle and was partially melted as if heat had been applied to it. Alongside was a cassette warped in a similar manner. The witness suffered from a severe migraine type headache after the two men left. His eyes also felt gritty and teary, and his face now appeared sunburned. He also suffered from strange dreams, one that was of lying prone on a table in a round room with a bright light above him, then sensing being touched.

Two days later, while going outside his house the witness saw the same two men he had seen before in the driveway. Both were dressed in white coveralls. One was carrying a Geiger counter, the other a twelve to sixteen inch parabolic dish in his hand, pointing to the sky, plus earphones and a microphone that was attached. He appeared to be searching the sky. The wires all led into a black box at his waist. At one point he had what looked like a camera, although not video, aimed at a tree over which the UFO had been originally seen. During the time they were together neither was seen speaking to each other. No car was seen which they might have arrived in.

In December, a few days after Christmas, a man appeared at the door of the witness. He stated that he had come to see his unusual watch. He stated that his name was Mr. Smith and showed some ID. He wore a dark charcoal suit, white shirt, and black tie. He also wore a black fedora. His feet were very large, 'size thirteen, or fourteen,' like the witness' previous visitors. His shoes were black and shiny, with no signs of dirt on them at all. He was about four-feet-eight-inches to five-feet tall, very thin, and very pale skinned with very long fingers. He also wore black wrap around glasses with silver frames. The witness extended his hand but was ignored (again).

Upon entering the house, the visitor commented upon the carved walking stick in the hallway. He also asked the witness to turn the microwave off before he walked in front of it. Sitting down at the kitchen table he produced a small silver tape recorder, claiming it could record up to eighty hours or more. Using a pick-like tool from his breast pocket he examined the witness' watch. He opened a black briefcase, removed some paper, a silver pencil with a red top, and a pen-like flash light that emitted a mauve, pencil thin beam, which he scanned the interior of the watch with. He took a small digital type camera and with it he took several pictures of the watch. During the whole of his visit he spoke very little, and his speech seemed slurred.

Again, the cats were agitated during the stranger's visit. He again expressed interest in the watch and the witness asked $500 for it, but he replied that he had to check with his colleagues. The stranger also expressed interest in a computer saying that it had very minimal power. The stranger departed without saying good-bye. The witness went immediately to the window but could not see any sign of the visitor or any car in the vicinity. He had simply vanished. A plastic hair blower nozzle was found melted and a ruler in a drawer close to where the visitor had been sitting was bent into a slight 'S' curve. Again, the witness suffered from a severe headache and an eruptive nosebleed.

In early January 2001, two peculiar strangers again visited the witness to the previous UFO encounter. These two were different from the others. They were at least six-feet tall, very bony, with head, hands and feet out of proportion to the rest of the body. They wore gray suits that seemed to be 'oily', had black ties and hats plus wrap-around sunglasses that they never took off. When questioned about the glasses they remarked that they could see perfectly well. Their ears stood out from their heads and their skin was pale white, whereas their fingernails were gray in color. They never removed the hats during their visit. And throughout the whole time only one of them spoke. When asked for ID's they displayed 'silver' cases that contained a photo with an unusual symbol, plus their names in small print.

Upon entering the kitchen, they asked the witness to please unplug the microwave. They also told him to turn the computer off. The two Persian cats were going crazy dashing around the room, and trying to get out of the window, which was closed. Each man carried a briefcase with an inverted 'L' shaped handle. The man that did all the talking asked to see the witness' unusual watch. He then removed from his briefcase four small containers, each had a different colored top. Opening two he proceeded to pour the contents over the watch. He told the concerned witness that no harm would come to the watch. He was given $250 for the watch and told that they would give him the rest later. He told them that he was moving soon, to this they replied; "We know. Don't worry, we can find you if we want to."

They soon departed without the common courtesies, staring blankly at the witness as he extended his hand. Once again, the witness hurried to the bedroom window only to find, as before, no sign of either man departing, nor could any vehicle be heard leaving. After the visit the witness felt drained, had a severe headache that lasted for two days and a rash on his arms, face and chest." GC

A READER FORWARDED the following account in May 2017:

"Hi Lon - I've been meaning to send you this story for some time now. It was one of the strangest events in my and my friend's life. This event took place approximately nineteen years ago, around 1998. A friend and I were on our way back to my place at about 2:00-2:30 a.m. one night coming from Exton, PA. We stopped at the Turkey Hill on RT 323 east of the town of Honey Brook to grab something to drink. I pulled into a parking space on the left side of the store in front of the window. I got out of the car, my friend remained in the car. Passing the window, I noticed a man leaning down on the window sill inside. He was wearing a wide-brimmed black hat and had his head down so I couldn't see his face, just the hat. Entering the store, I noticed the male clerk behind the counter with his back to me. I retrieved the drinks I went in for and proceeded to the counter. As I did, I observed the man leaning down in the sill, head still down, wearing all black and a black trench coat. Paying for my items I noticed that the clerk acted as if the man wasn't even there, but slightly spooked at the same time.

Leaving the store, I intended to relay this to my friend

waiting in my car. As I got back in, she was looking at the man leaning down in the sill and asked if I see this guy. I said yes and had told her a little about being inside the store as I put the car in reverse to leave. At that point the man began to raise his head, he faced directly out at us, but oddly, as my friend yelled, he had no face! It was like it was blurred out, like they do on TV. Needless to say, we were both freaked out a little and I tore off out of the lot and headed east toward my home which was only a quarter mile or so from the store. My friend and I were silent at this point as I pulled into the entrance of my mobile home park. I stopped the car there and told my friend we were going back as I suspected the clerk may be getting robbed by the man in the window. We headed out of the entrance and back to the store.

I decided to make a right on a back road across from the store, by a local store/deli and told my friend to look over inside the store to see what she could. The man was no longer crouching in the sill but couldn't be seen inside anywhere either. I proceeded a short distance down this road to turn around when we witnessed a female, wearing all black, walking towards us in the middle of the opposite lane. After passing her I immediately turned around to head back toward the store and ask the female if she needed help. Reaching the stop sign at the intersection we noticed she was gone. We then turned our attention back to the store across the street and decided to go right, heading west on 322, We drove slowly past the store when we noticed the man was now outside, crouching by the pay phone, head down, to the right of the store, and a blacked out Lincoln continental or town car parked to his left that we hadn't noticed before. The clerk was inside standing behind the counter at this point staring straight out the windows and perfectly still.

I turned around a short distance down at the next mobile

home park with the small diner in front and proceeded east again. This time we pulled back into the parking lot. The man, the car, and the clerk still in the same positions as previous. The man began raising his head again, and again, I tore off out of the lot, going east on 322 toward my home. About three hundred feet from leaving the lot I had to swerve to miss another man, wearing all black, walking towards us, in the center of our lane, going west towards the store. Both mine, and my friend's hearts were pounding at this point and again, I had to turn around and go back, wondering what the hell was going on.

As we returned back to the store and pulled into the lot we noticed that the walking man was gone, the crouching man with no face was gone, and the car was gone. The male clerk from inside, was now a female clerk moving around doing work inside the store. At no time did we witness any other patrons to the store, nor any other vehicles in the lot during any of this.

After finally returning home, and talking for a bit, my friend calmed down enough to drive herself home. Passing the store after leaving, the same female clerk was still the only person there. My friend's car subsequently broke down on her a short distance away. She did make it home safe that night though. I frequented that same store, and days later saw that same male clerk working there where I noticed his demeanor to be totally different from that night.

Neither of us at the time thought we had witnessed Men in Black activity. It wasn't until years later while researching stories of MIB encounters that it hit me. We have both seen unidentified craft periodically throughout our lives, and she, and her mother, have witnessed a being that didn't seem of this Earth. We still keep in contact to this day. Because of a landed unidentified craft my mother witnessed in the late 1970s

*when I was about 8 or 9, I've researched events involving
UFOs throughout my life and attempt to investigate sightings
now." Michael*

This is one of more bizarre MIB encounters I have read. A
multi-faceted incident with a faceless MIB, a female MIB and a
possible time slip. Why they were there in the first place? The
area is known for UFO activity, so that may be the answer.

I RECEIVED the following account in January 2018:

*"I knew a dude who worked at the Experimental Mines - US
Bureau of Mines (western Pennsylvania). It's an interesting
place with twelve foot double row barbed wire fence all
around it, and it's pretty good size. Located at 40°18'21.9"N
79°58'49.2"W.*

*Anyway, there were four of us riding around aimlessly in
one dude's car. We were kids, nineteen or twenty, all off work,
driving around drinking beer and smoking joints, just having
fun. We drove past the mines and saw the one gate was open.
So, we turned around and decided to check it out. There was
no guard in the booth, so we drove right on in, and up a hill,
around a bend. Then suddenly a dark blue Caprice Classic cut
us off and stopped. A white Caprice Classic pulled up behind
us. Two seemingly identical 'men' wearing black suits with
black ties, and black sunglasses approached the car. I don't
remember seeing which one got out of which car. They were
just there, one on either side of us. The one on the left said;
"State your business here." We said we saw the gate standing
open and our buddy works here, so we came in to see if we
could find him. He said; "You have no business here. This is a*

restricted area."We repeated that the gate was standing wide open and added that there was no guard there. He said; "You will follow me." He then walked very quickly to the car in front of us. The one on the right of us never said a word. He got in the car behind us.

We followed the blue car, with the white car behind us, around a loop road and back out thru the same, still open gate. The blue car pulled over next to the empty guard booth. The white car followed us to the next intersection, maybe half a mile, and turned off. We hauled ass. Never saw that gate open again after that. It scared the crap out of us. It's a creepy looking place in the first place. The fences make it look like a prison complex. Why would they need such intense security at a coal mine? This was long before 9/11; like 1983/84. Our buddy was a janitor, he didn't have access to the whole complex, just the offices he took care of. He said there was a lot of weird things going on there. Mean-looking men and women with sunglasses indoors. Guarded buildings. Army trucks. Chevy Caprice Classics, all either black, dark blue, or white.

He was particularly creeped out by one woman there. He didn't want to clean her office, another guy had to do it. This is going by what he said, I have no firsthand knowledge of it. I can tell you that the whole surrounding area has a weird vibe going on. There are neighborhoods bordering the complex on three sides, and woods is across the road. This wasn't the first paranormal event in my life, nor was it the last, but I shared this one with three other people. I haven't spoken to any of them in years. Don't even know where they live now. But I know they saw the same thing I did."

As of 1999, the complex is made up of lab and office space as part of the National Energy Technology Laboratory network. It is also home to three major agencies including the Federal Energy Technology Center (US Department of

Energy), the National Institute for Occupational Safety and Health (US Department of Health and Human Services, Centers for Disease Control), and the Mine Safety & Health Administration (US Department of Labor). Before that time,

I have no idea what was going on at the location, other than earlier when there was CDC / NIOSH mine research. Quite a bizarre encounter.

I ALSO RECEIVED this next account in January 2018:

"I came across one of your articles where someone asked if it was OK to confront the MIB if you encounter them. I would not recommend it. I had two encounters with them, and I do expect to have another.

They are very strange. I will not say they are agents from some government agency or from another 'whatever.' My encounter resulted from an incident that I had a few months earlier, but that is a whole different story that does not belong here.

My first encounter was at my home. They came to my front door. How they got past the security gate and cameras is beyond me, but they did it. The first thing they said to me when I opened the door was; "You did not see what you think you saw!"

It was obvious they were trying to intimidate me, and this made me angry. I told them to get off my property and not come back. They said nothing, just turned slowly and walked away down my driveway. Three weeks later I was driving on the highway in another state on a long straight section doing about sixty-five miles per hour. A car came up next to me and as I looked at the car there they were. The passenger just sat *there staring at me with no facial expression at all. I sped up to about eighty miles per hour and they just pulled up next to me and stayed there. I basically slammed on my brakes, they just kept going, and to date I have not seen them again. I believe they were showing me they can find you whenever and wherever they decide to do so.*

I did notice that they projected arrogance, uncaring emotions but mostly total intimidation. It was their attempt to intimidate me that made me angry because I have always refused to live under threats or perceived threats. However, I do think they are or could be dangerous. My advice to others is to just try to ignore them if possible. Be aware and be careful."
HO

I'd say that this is good advice. Intimidation does seem to be their main objective. But I also believe that they could become extremely dangerous if they need to be. It's obvious that some of these MIB possess certain otherworldly and unpleasant abilities.

I RECENTLY FOUND the next account on one of my older databases:

"This is such a bizarre incident I'm about to describe to you. I can't be certain, but this most likely occurred in the summer of 1992 which would have been the summer before my senior year in high school. I was hanging out in the driveway at my best friend's house on N. Greenfield Ave. in Waukesha, WI. It was about 4 p.m. I had parked my 1980 Chevy Malibu on the curb in front of his house.

As my best friend and I were standing in the driveway, a

brand-new black Lincoln Town Car with tinted windows pulled up behind my car, blocking the driveway. As soon as it stopped, three men including the driver got out of the car. They walked up to the sidewalk and faced us. They were all wearing black suits and dark tinted sunglasses; all of them normal build and physically fit.

The strangest part about the incident was that the one man immediately addressed me, as if he knew the Malibu was my car. "I will give you $2000 cash for your car." He was, as far as I can remember, totally expressionless, as were the others. As I understood, he would hand me cash and drive the car away immediately. It didn't seem like a transfer of the title was an issue. Still kind of confused by the offer, the only thing that I managed to say was; "It's not mine to sell. My dad owns it," which was true. That was it. They made no more attempts to make a deal. They turned around without a word, got into their car and drove away. They didn't stop at any other houses as far as we could see.

At the time I knew nothing of Men in Black incidents nor did my friend. We both stood there confounded and after talking about what had happened, we came to the conclusion that $2000 would have been a great deal for me, but not worth the possible hassle that may have followed. Strangely enough my dad sold the car a few weeks later. I think he got less than $500 for it.

My friend can back up my claim. I haven't seen him for almost five years, but it was such an odd event. We reminisced on it a few times after it happened. I always wondered if other so-called Men in Black had ever approached people and offered to buy their cars or any other property." MM

There have been other instances when a MIB would seem enamored with a piece of property and make a cash offer for it;

especially jewelry and small appliances; it's just another odd aspect of the MIB phenomenon.

IN 1947, a UFO eyewitness named Harold Dahl claimed to have been warned not to talk about his alleged sighting on Maury Island in Puget Sound by a man in a dark suit. In the mid-1950s, the influential Ufologist Albert K. Bender claimed he was visited by men in dark suits who threatened and warned him not to continue investigating UFOs. Bender maintained that the men in black were secret government agents who had been given the task of suppressing evidence of UFOs. John A. Keel claimed to have had personal encounters with the Men in Black and referred to them as 'demonic supernaturals' with "dark skin and/or exotic facial features." There have also been claims that the entire phenomenon was fabricated in order to enhanced earlier UFO-based stories.

Whatever you believe, the MIBs have become an important part of the UFO genre. These beings have been seen and recorded for almost seventy years. I have no doubt that the phenomenon will continue and mostly likely evolve into the future.

12

ENCOUNTERS THAT DEFY
EXPLANATION

EXPERIENCERS HAVE ENCOUNTERED a variety of unexplained beings and humanoids; all, of which, are an enigma.
Humans have given many of these non-terrestrials identifying
names (ex. Greys, Reptilians, Nordics, etc.) based on physical
characteristics. Nonetheless, we still know very little about
them. But there are some beings and related encounters that
simply defy explanation. In some cases, we are fortunate to
receive photographs or sketches from an experiencer. I'm not
saying that this evidence helps to identify the unknown being,
but it can give us an idea of what the eyewitness encountered
and why they reacted in a certain manner.

I received the following information and image (above) from
UFO investigator Ken Pfeifer. It was forwarded to Ken by one
of his readers; then sent to me so it could be published:

*"In November 2012, I was working the night shift on an x-ray
crew at a material gas plant. This was around 3 a.m. and there
was only four of us in the plant at the time. I took the included
photograph after seeing something swaying side to side out of
the corner of my eye. I was in the basket of a descending man-*

lift when I took the photo. By the time I unhooked my harness to get out of the basket the creature was gone.

The police were called, and they walked premises. The officer told me there were 26 UFO sighting calls throughout that night. I have no doubt of what I saw that night. The other person that saw it with me took off running for the truck."
Darryl

I contacted the witness directly, and received this follow-up:

"You can use my name and the picture was taken near Kenedy, TX. I appreciate the quick reply. The picture was even printed in the local newspaper in Kenedy. I had sent the picture to the officer who came to the plant and assume he sent it to the newspaper. Thanks." Darryl

A FEW MONTHS LATER, I received another account from a witness in Texas:

"To the editor - I live near Beeville, Texas and want to report an incident from a few weeks ago. It was about 9:30 p.m. when I heard 'swishing' sounds coming from outside. I went to the back door in the kitchen and looked out. My yard was illuminated, so I walked outside onto the porch and suddenly noticed a wide disc-shaped craft hovering above the house. It was at least 100-foot wide. In an instant I was hit by a beam of light and lifted off the top step of the porch. I was mid-air for almost twenty seconds, then slowly set down by the side of the tool barn. I was very groggy; almost like I was drunk.

I then noticed a figure moving out of a beam of blue light that came directly from below the craft. This figure was about five foot tall and looked human, but the extremities and head looked as though it had been burned and charred. It reminded me of a zombie from TV. It moved closer to me. I was literally frozen stiff. As it got closer, I became nauseated. It looked awful and had a putrid odor. It backed away as I started to wretch, then vanished into the blue beam of light. Without hesitation, the craft ascended swiftly; so fast that it created an instant vacuum that dropped me to my knees.

I got to my feet and ran into the house. I was scared and worried something else may happen. Then I noticed the time. It was 10:40 p.m. I had lost almost one hour of time. I still don't understand what happened to me or the time. I feel fine but I'm still very concerned. I never believed in UFOs or other weird experiences people have said they had. Now it has happened to me and I have a deep sense of dread. I talked to my close friend and she told me to search the internet. I don't know if she believed me, but she was willing to help. To be frank, I am still concerned about contacting anyone about this.

My friend gave me several contacts to try. I sent emails and filled a few forms. I never heard back from any of them. Then I found the photo of the entity from Kenedy, TX that was posted on your blog. That is what I encountered. I know that it is the same thing or another like it. I can feel it deep inside me. That gas plant in Kenedy is only 20 miles from me!

Just yesterday, there was some talk that weird looking people were seen moving through a local field this past weekend. There was also a series of lights seen above the horizon at the same location. I don't know if this is related.

Can you get back to me? I really need some answers." - *Name withheld by request of the witness*

I called the witness at her place of business the next morning. She hesitantly described the incident and asked if I could answer questions. I don't know if what she witnessed was the same entity from the March 2013 incident in Kenedy, Texas, but it's an interesting possibility.

The witness lives alone. Her close friend lives nearby, about a quarter mile away. I received permission to publish her ordeal in hope of getting others to come forward. The witness is terrified that this entity will return. Because there is an issue of lost time, I mentioned regressive hypnosis; but this is not the best option for everyone. She doesn't appear to have any ill-effects from the encounter, but I recommended that she closely monitor her health and seek care if anything unusual starts to surface. The witness gave me permission to make these statements.

FOR ALMOST SIX YEARS, I followed and documented the exploits of my friend and colleague JC Johnson of Crypto 4 Corners. Unfortunately, for all of us, JC passed away in 2018. We had talked about me writing a book about his investigations and encounters, which I may consider doing in the future. In the meantime, I wanted to add two of JC's otherworldly observations.

There was an incident April 2014 that involved a Navajo family group and other residents living in a non-specific location in the vicinity of Gallup, New Mexico. According the witnesses, Bradford and Maria, a series of gunshots and heavy ground artillery could be heard and felt from the distance. Soon after, bright beams of light appeared from above their Hogan (a traditional Navajo hut). The lights were so bright that it illuminated the inside of their domicile through the windows and, incredibly, through tiny cracks in the walls and ceiling. The lights seemed to cause disorientation, but the witnesses were able to tell that the beams came from a honey-combed shaped array from a craft hovering above.

The witnesses made their way towards the main house behind the hogan. As they were running, they noticed a saucer-shaped craft hovering over the house with multi-colored lights rotating around it. The beams were displaying from different directions from other nondescript craft. These craft were creating torrents of strong wind that literally pushed the pinon and juniper trees to the ground. The witnesses also noticed very small entities scurrying around the enclosed dogs, suddenly causing the dogs to stop barking and become rendered unconscious.

At the same time, Bradford stated that his uncle was battling an entity at his house nearby. It became apparent that the uncle either incapacitated or killed the being.

Bradford and other residents in the area started to confront the craft with personal firearms. At one point, Bradford was discharging his AK-47 at the craft when the weapon started to 'heat up' to the point that Bradford had to set it down because it was becoming too hot to hold. He states, 'something' from the craft directed itself onto the weapon.

It is interesting to note that some of the elderly residents were yelling at the craft; "Go back to the stars."

Back in the house, the witnesses described hearing footsteps on the roof, as well scampering outside on the ground. They were making desperate calls to 911 and local authorities.

When the fire department and state police started to arrive, the craft started moving away. Someone from the fire department stated that, "They could see bright headlights on the roof", as they made their way to the location. There were four state police cruisers on the scene, as well as an unknown individual in a black Cadillac Escalade SUV. The witness referred to this man as a 'universal soldier' decked out in flack gear and armed to the teeth. This person never said a word, but it was obvious that the state police knew who he was, and they were taking directions (through hand signals) from him as well.

When this 'universal soldier' overheard the witness statement describing his uncle's encounter with one of the entities, he immediately made a beeline to the uncle's residence. The SUV was driven to the uncle's house and very soon something was carried out of the house and placed into an unknown vessel (possibly cryogenic) in the SUV. Not long after, JC Johnson was contacted by Navajo Criminal Investigations in reference to the incident. He investigated the incident and then relayed the information to me.

Earlier in the book, I mentioned that I didn't believe that BEKs and black-eyed people could be classified as alien beings. That being stated, there was an encounter, involving JC Johnson and Jack Cary, that went a bit beyond the standard BEK fare.

During a June 2014 follow-up investigation of the alien encounter case, JC Johnson and his colleague Jack Cary encountered something that neither can explain. The incident occurred in the high desert around Gallup, New Mexico.

JC and Jack were in the backseat of a vehicle driven by a resident of the reservation, who was also accompanied by an acquaintance. The group was traveling on a dirt road on the high desert, along a rail line, searching for evidence related to the other case.

As they were observing the area from the car, they noticed an unidentified figure ahead of them. As they got closer, JC and Jack witnessed a female, seemingly in her late teens exiting the brush. The driver slowed the vehicle, though neither passenger in the front seemed to be uneasy or concerned by the presence of the female. In fact, they were busy talking to each other according to JC.

The description given by JC and Jack was not typical of what someone would expect in this isolated location. The female was Caucasian and had an attractive face and figure. Her face and hair were clean, though she was wearing 6-inch cork heels (wedge) and a filthy, tattered one-piece denim jumpsuit.

JC asked if she was "OK," in which she replied "I'm fine. I have everything I need." As she looked directly at JC and Jack, they were both stunned by what they saw.

Her eyes were completely black in color; projecting evil and malice according to both witnesses. Immediately JC became disoriented and told the driver to leave now! Jack became violently ill, almost to the point of throwing up. They both implored that they leave. The driver seemed to be unaware of what had happened. JC stated that he was totally confused as they eventually sped away and that his head was 'burning' like an oven. Jack possesses spiritual healing abilities and attempted to alleviate some of JC's discomfort by transferring the pain through him. At the time, this greatly reduced JC's suffering, but led to several days of anguish for Jack.

After traveling several miles from the location, they stopped the vehicle and got out to revitalize themselves. Oddly enough, JC looked back in the direction they had come from and noticed the same figure in the distance walking towards them. They quickly got into the car and continued on their way.

JC continued to experience bouts of disorientation for many months. There was some indication that there may have been a possible spiritual malevolence that contributed in this incident, but JC maintained that he believed something else was involved. He never discounted alien activity because of his association with the previous case.

IN OCTOBER 2012, I received the following account from Steve Ririe who, at the time, had lived in Las Vegas, NV for over fifty years. He has worked in various capacities in the US Government and was referred to me by a local UFO investigator and colleague. I have examined Steve's credentials and believe him to be quite credible:

"What you are about to read is a little weird. Correction; it's a lot weird. But, for whatever reason, I felt it was interesting enough to write down. Keep in mind, there are first-hand stories, second-hand stories and so on. This is a third-hand story with as little poetic license as necessary. I am confident I have recorded the details with a high degree of accuracy. It may get confusing but here we go.

What I know of this story came from my close friend named Doug. I have known Doug for many years. He is a successful businessman and I would never question his integrity. Several months ago, Doug came by my office and while we visited, he related the details of a conversation he had with one of his long-time customers. To be honest, Doug and I both don't know what to make to this strange conversation with his customer. His story may just be the raving of a schizophrenic. And although the credibility of the person who shared their first-hand account with Doug would make a diagnosis of schizophrenia difficult to imagine, that would at least make sense. But it's an interesting story, nonetheless. After writing it down, I emailed the story to Doug for verification. He confirmed I had written the account down as accurately as he felt possible. With that introduction, here is what Doug told me.

I have this customer that sat down with me at my office and posed a very strange question. He asked; "Do you believe in UFO's?" I have only known him for a short time, but I do know he was in the US Marine Corps and he has enough accolades and credentials that I would not question his integrity. He comes across extremely reputable which made his story both intriguing and bizarre.

In order to protect his identity, and since I do not have his permission to relate this story, I will refer to him as John.

I told John that I, of course, do believe there are things that have been seen flying and at the same time been unidentifiable. What I don't know is what they were, since, of course, they are by their very nature unidentifiable. That is as logical of a statement as I could have made. John appeared to have accepted my answer. He took it as an affirmative, which is to say that I do in fact believe in UFO's. Crossing that bridge, the strange story began to unroll out of John's mouth. The following is the story told by John to my friend Doug.

The story John shared revolved around an elderly friend that lived close to him. I will call his elderly friend Tom. One day Tom asked John if, in fact, he believed in UFO's. John answered in the affirmative. Tom proceeded. He said he had something he wanted to show John. But first, prior to sharing his story, he must take John to a site in Las Vegas.

Once the evening had settled in and the sun had long disappeared behind the Red Rock Mountains the two of them drove to the corner of Tropicana and Decatur Blvd., just a few miles west from the Las Vegas Strip. This site is well known by long-time Vegas residents that live on the west side of the city. The name it is known by is 'the Pits.' Due to its strange and varied dirt mounds it is favored by dirt bike enthusiasts. And although it is not far from the famous Las Vegas Strip, it remained undeveloped due to several reasons. The first would be the cost of leveling the ground and the second would be its location being part of a major wash heading into Las Vegas. The City of Las Vegas has contended *for years with flash floods and washes are not the best sites to develop.*

When they arrived at the Pits they pulled off into the desert and walked to a spot where Tom indicated they should stop. Tom began surveying the area with what John assumed was a metal detector. After some searching, he found a spot where the detector came alive. He placed a rock at that point. Then he went off in another direction until the detector sounded again. Another rock was placed at the second point. Again, he repeated his search for a spot in the dark that would complete an equilateral triangle. Sure enough, the detector sounded at the exact spot. He placed a third rock. All the time searching and setting up the triangle, Tom kept checking his watch.

With all three corners of the triangle revealed, he began to feel his way to the true center of the triangle. Judging his position relative to the three points of the triangle and feeling confident he was in position, he stepped aside and placed John dead center in the triangle. Tom stepped back staring at his watch and waited. "John," he said. "In just a minute you will feel a pulse through your body. The points of the triangle are places where transmission pillars have been buried deep in the Earth. In the center of these transmission pillars, where you now stand, is where the transmission waves will generate. Where they are transmitting to, I don't know. But I do know these transmissions occur at regular intervals during the late night. And when they occur you can feel them. They are about to transmit any minute now." They both remained quiet as they waited. Suddenly, just as Tom had described, John felt a sensation in the darkness.

John described a physical force like an electrical pulse rolling up his body from his toes to his head. It was as if a group of people were surrounding you with rolling pins and they were rolling them up your body from your toes to the top of your head. It didn't last too long and just as suddenly as it started, it stopped. It was never made clear to John how Tom knew about these transmission events. He was only told that, for whatever reason, Tom had known about certain alien information for many years and was sworn to secrecy. With that experience under John's belt, Tom felt confident that John was prepared for what Tom felt compelled to show him. The only reason Tom gave for showing John any of this was; "Just in case."

Next Tom took John on a drive outside of Las Vegas. They headed west on the Blue Diamond Hwy leading toward Pahrump, Nevada. The town of Blue Diamond is about fifteen to twenty miles southwest of Las Vegas. At some point near Blue Diamond, Tom drove off the highway and headed into the desert. Tom told him that what he was about to show him he needed to get off his chest. He had information about aliens among us and was sworn to secrecy. He had kept these secrets for as long as he could, which John assumed was many years. At Tom's advanced age he wanted someone else to know some of what he knew. The headlights bounced in front of their car illuminating the dirt road that led deeper into the desert. As cacti and sagebrush rushed passed them Tom confessed that by "spilling the beans" his life would be in danger. Regardless of the consequences for both of them they drove on. Moments later they pulled up to a door in the middle of nowhere set into the side of a rocky bluff. This door, this location, this place, was what Tom wanted John to see. They only stayed a moment when Tom said; "We have to leave right now. They know we are here."

As they drove away from the mysterious door, suddenly lights which appeared to them as headlights materialized virtually out of nowhere and began following them. Tom picked up speed. At several points the lights tailed them no less than three feet off their back bumper. Jolts of anxiety, fear, and panic swept through both Tom and John. Without warning the lights went black. Tom craned his neck to look back. No lights or vehicle were visible, only darkness.

That was the last time John would see Tom. Days after this strange experience, John sought Tom out but was unable to find him. Tom's home was empty and none of his neighbors knew where he went. None of them saw him leave. The neighbor across the street claimed to see men in white hazmat suits take all Tom's belongings.

After several days, not being able to move past the strange events, John decided he would revisit the transmission site. Late one evening, while driving home from work, he made a detour to the Pits. As he approached, he anticipated pulling into the desert area where he and Tom had once parked. He discovered that he wouldn't be able to pull off the road due to a dirt berm having been erected. He instead parked his truck on the shoulder of the road and got out. He made his way to the berm and climbed up. Instead of the dark vacant area he had visited days before, now before him was a lot of construction equipment and massive construction lights flooding the entire area. He climbed up the berm and, while resting on his stomach, looked over to see what all the commotion was about. No sooner had he began looking when suddenly, as if on cue, flood lights all around the construction site turned and pointed their beams directly at his position. Not wanting to feel paranoid he quickly left the area and drove home. Later he learned the city had started construction on a flood retention basin and park at the site.

John still couldn't shake the feelings left by this experience. Where was Tom? Considering what was going on at the transmission site, did any of it have to do with Tom? Eventually, he shared the experience to a couple of his friends.

They, of course, were curious and wanted him to show them the door in the desert. After some coaxing, John agreed, and they headed out. They took his friend's vehicle and John sat shotgun. At one point, as they were driving the dirt road, John began to feel nervous and admittedly scared. He considered telling his friend to take a wrong turn, acting as though he had forgotten the directions how to get there. He knew had he acted as if he didn't remember the location of the door, he'd take a lot of heat from his friends. Instead of deflecting, he found himself drawn closer in the direction of the door. His own curiosity had gotten the best of him.

As they drove along, they saw up ahead an old pickup truck that had pulled off alongside the dirt road. As they approached, they could make out an extremely tall thin man leaning against the driver's side door. His dress was casual, and he sported a pair of dark sunglasses. They pulled up behind the truck and the tall man walked up to the driver's window, bent down and asked them what they were doing out there.

"We're just driving around," said the driver and they all gestured in the affirmative.

"You need to turn around," he told them. "You've driven on to private property."

"Who are you?" they said, pushing back with a little attitude, not willing to immediately comply.

"I'm the law out here," he said, but he wore no uniform, nor did he flash a badge. The tall man offered no sign of authority. John's friends were unimpressed.

The tall man straightened, paused, then slowly walked around the vehicle and lowered his head into the passengers' window where John sat. John's window was down. When he was face to face with John, he raised his sunglasses and look directly into his eyes. What John saw in the tall man's eyes

216

sent a shock throughout his entire body. Looking back at him were not the eyes of a man. The tall man's eyes were more feline than human, and he addressed John by his full name. "John Blank," he said. "Consider this your warning. Do we have an understanding?"

John said, "Yes." And with that they drove away.

That is the extent of the story as told by John to my friend Doug. I don't know any more. I have lived in Las Vegas for over fifty years and have never seen a door in the desert. But there are parts of the desert around Blue Diamond that are not accessible to the public.

Doug has approached John since talking to me and asked if he would be willing to take us to the door. So far, the answer is; "No." SR The tall man could have been a being similar to a MIB, though the feline-like eyes are an interesting caveat.

THE NEXT ACCOUNT was forwarded to me in February 2013:

"This past Monday night I was driving home from work around 9:45 p.m. I live in a very rural area south of Falls Village, CT and I was only two miles from my residence. The roads were still slick from the heavy snow we had received, so I was driving very deliberately. All at once, a deer jumped from behind a snow bank and bolted in front of my car. I slammed on the brakes but still skidded into the back of the deer. I didn't see where the deer went, but I was now stuck in the snow bank. I got out of the car and noticed that my driver's side headlight was smashed. I tried to push the car out the snow

bank, but it was not budging. So, I had no choice other than to call for a tow truck.

About 15 minutes after I called for help, one of my neighbors was on his way home and stopped to ask if he could help. I told him I had called for a tow truck, but I didn't know how long it be before it 170 showed up. He said that he would go home, grab some chains and return with his four-wheel drive pickup in order to pull me out. I thanked him and he left.

Not long after my neighbor left, I noticed lights coming toward me on the road. The lights were large and very bright, so I figured that it was the tow truck. As the lights slowly proceeded towards me, several more lights illuminated above and below the others. The vehicle, or whatever it was, stopped about 50 yards from me and remained there for several minutes. Then all of a sudden, I witnessed a brightly lit 'being' floating through the woods across from me. It reminded me of those bright white aliens from the 'Cocoon' movie though I didn't see any facial features. This being quickly floated through the trees then out onto the road. It started to come towards me, but I was petrified. I just could not move. It didn't have arms or legs but there was definitely a head and something on the end that resembled a fish tail. It stopped directly in front of me and hovered no more than ten feet away. There were no eyes or mouth, but I did feel warmth coming from it. It was very calming and comforting. Then it suddenly whisked towards the lights. After a few minutes the bright lights started to fade until it was completely gone.

My neighbor soon returned, as well as the tow truck operator. I asked them both if they had noticed any vehicle with intense bright lights, but they both looked at me like I was crazy. After they pulled me from the snow bank I drove home, quickly took a bath and headed for bed. I was still feeling a calming sensation and desperately wanted to go to sleep.

I was off work on Tuesday, so I decided to go and have my headlight fixed. As I approached the area where I had been stuck the night before, I noticed that the area where the lights were, was completely barren of snow and the roadway was dry. Did I have an alien close encounter? To be honest with you, I don't believe in UFOs, aliens or any of that weird stuff. But I am having second thoughts as to what I witnessed. Was it simply a spirit of some kind? I have had dealings with ghosts and spirits since I was young. What is your opinion?" Beth

I called and asked Beth why she would believe in spiritual beings but not believe in alien beings. She witnessed enough evidence to form a fairly reasonable evaluation. In my opinion and experience, there is a fine line between spirits and non-terrestrial beings. In some cases, these beings could be interpreted as the same type of entity. I think Beth has awoken to a greater sense of truth, that we're not alone.

———

THIS NEXT INTERESTING account was sent to me in February 2013:

"Hello, I'm writing you in an effort to confirm an unusual observation I had on October 16, 2012 at around 11:15 p.m. I was driving home from work northbound on RT 20, West Ridge Rd. near Fairview, PA when I notice bright green lights descending into the woods behind a veterinary hospital. I immediately slowed and pulled into the lot behind the hospital. I could see several green lights in the woods and a few red and white lights. I got out of the car to get a better view. As I stood in front of my car, I started to hear distinct 'chopping' sounds coming from the woods as well as cracking noises. It

actually sounded like several people were cutting down trees. The lights and the activity were about fifty yards in front of me but I couldn't see any movement.

I stood there for about ten minutes as the sounds continued. I was tired so I decided to leave for home. I figured that there were workers clearing land though this was near a residential location and working at night was a bit unusual.

As I made my way back into the car, I noticed movement in an adjacent parking lot. The lot was lit enough to where I could see two figures moving away from me towards the woods. They looked like characters from a cartoon. The figures were about five foot tall, light in color and very thin. I couldn't see their faces, but the heads had a peanut shape. They move swiftly but only their legs were moving. Every other parts of their bodies were rigid. There was also a white sash tied across the waist on both figures.

As I watched the figures move into the woods, a whirling sound starting to come from the same area. Suddenly five huge green lights ascended from the woods, hovered for a second or two, then vanished. I think that the lights stretched out for about one hundred and fifty feet. It was a very large craft.

The next day I walked through the woods where this incident occurred and noticed a few small trees in a particular area were cracked near the ground. There was nothing else out of the ordinary.

I decided not to mention what I witnessed and see if anyone had reported it to the local media. As of today, I have not seen any mention of this landing or the lights. I live in Fairview, PA and have not heard any mention from any resident. I rather not have my particulars disclosed at least until another similar report is made public. This is a small town, and everybody is in everyone else's business, if you know what I mean.

Would you be kind enough to let me know of any reports in my area? Thank you." RS

After receiving the email, I found a strange report in the MUFON CMS. It came from a truck driver who had been in the same general area and the descriptions of the beings were somewhat similar. I'm not sure if these two incidents were related, even though the event occurred within three months of each other.

THE FOLLOWING narrative was recently found in one of my older databases:

"In 1993, my brother and I had a run in with a small human-like being with bright yellow eyes. We live on an old ranch outside of Austin, Texas. My brother and I are twins; we were 16-years-old at the time. We were working in the barn at dusk and my brother noticed a pair of yellow eyes peeking out of a gully near the creek. We both watched for a minute or two until it appeared again. I grabbed a shotgun that was on the work table and we made our way towards this thing.

We stood still about fifty feet away from the gully when suddenly this little human-like thing scampered out toward the creek. I took a shot at it (double-odd buckshot) but it kept on running. This thing looked like it walked across the creek surface. The craziest thing I'd ever seen. It made its way to the other side and disappeared into a field. It was 2-foot-tall or so with dark hairless skin. The eyes were so bright; almost like yellow colored pen lights.

We both told our parents and friends who all thought we were nuts. That brings us to a recent event.

Our parents have since passed away and my brother and I own most of the original ranch property. We are both married with families. We also built houses on the old property.

This past spring my brother and I were clearing some bushes and trees behind my house. It was around 8:30 p.m. and we were starting to douse the burning brush pile. Something caught my eye towards the onion field opposite the creek. It looked like a quick flash of bright light. My brother didn't see it. My wife came running out of the house and yelled that she saw something land in the field. She had been on the 2nd floor and saw it from the bedroom window.

The three of us watched in that direction for several minutes. We didn't notice anything unusual. We finished up and went into the house. I couldn't sleep that night. My wife said that the object was egg-shaped and descended quickly; so fast that she expected it to crash.

The next day, I walked through the field but didn't see anything out of the ordinary.

I'm concerned that something unusual is going on. We used to see coyotes, deer, wild birds and other wildlife frequently. But since the last incident, none of us have seen anything. Birds don't fly over or land on the property. There are several large oak trees on the property, but there has been significant die off. It not 'oak wilt' or insects. The leaves just die and fall off. It's very strange. I had the guy from the local nursery look around, but he can't explain it." SG

There have been accounts of unexplained beings and/or UFO activity that would render some land area unusable or toxic. I hadn't heard back from the eyewitness, so I have no idea how long the phenomenon continued.

A READER RECALLED A VERY unusual incident witnessed by his mother and several of her family members:

"My mother and her family were working in Naples, Florida in the late 1950s. One dayworker saw something crash nearby. A plane? All the workers ran to the site to search for survivors. The aircraft was sticking out of the sea near the beach. When the rescue got there, they realize it wasn't a plane, but some type of unknown craft.

The 'ship' had no doors or windows that could be seen. Beside the ship was one of the pilots. The pilot was still in its bizarre suit. It was tall and skinny, and wearing a very large helmet. The helmet didn't have a shield, but it did have a robotic looking face plate. Two of the workers picked it up and said it had little weight. It appeared to be dead. Others found a second suit. The suit was empty. It was laying in the nearby grass. Still others tried to get into the ship to look for any other survivors.

Then suddenly, an Army helicopter appeared. The Army came in great numbers to secure the location. Troops surrounded the workers' camp and force them to stay. They were there for two days afterward. The military told the workers that no one would believe them if they told what had transpired. One commander told them; "Who would believe hobos, drunks, and uneducated Mexicans?" The foreman told the workers to do what the military said, and no one would get hurt.

While trapped there, my mother observed the whole situation. On one of the two days trapped there, she met an unusual person. While sitting waiting for the occupation to be over, a person wearing a large blanket approached her from behind. In a bizarre mechanical voice, the strange individual asked her, "Are they looking for me?" She turned to see a mechanical face under the blanket. There appeared to be lips moving but there was a delay of sound coming from them. She realized it was not human and told it; "Yes" She told it to keep away from the military and look for a chance to escape.

There is a happy ending to this story. When the Army was still there cleaning up, some of the workers helped the surviving crew member. They put a hooded coat on it and other clothes to totally cover it up. They poured booze over it to make it smell like a drunk and helped it since it had trouble walking. When the bus came to pick up a batch of workers, the workers carried it onto the bus. It suddenly spoke with its mechanical voice; "Are they still looking for me?" They told it to shut up and get on the bus. The family left the next day. Those who took the alien were never seen again." T-Bear

I was able to talk to the witness' son, who swore that the account was true. He said that his mother would never lie about something like this. I just wonder whatever became of the surviving entity.

⸻

I RECEIVED an inquiry in February 2016, from an elderly woman in the Phoenix suburb of Surprise, Arizona. She states that she witnessed two humanoid beings standing outside her bedroom window a few days before Christmas 2015. The following report includes most of the information from the incident, though there are a few personal notes that I have redacted. I called and talked to the witness the next day in an attempt to gather more details.

I sketched a rendering of one of the beings from the description offered by the witness. She concurred that this is what she witnessed. The following statement is from her initial email.

"Hello Mr. Strickler. Feb. 10, 2016, around 12-21 or 12-22-2015, I woke up about 1:30 a.m. I glanced out my bedroom window, and this is what I saw: Two grayish-brown short people like figures with cone heads. The tallest stood approximately four foot tall, and the smallest one about three foot stood directly in front of the taller one. They stood motionless. I looked, then looked again, as I have never seen anything like this ever! I set on the edge of my bed and I just kept looking at them. They didn't move. Neither one of them had facial features at all. It appeared to me they had something over their heads to hide their appearance. I didn't let my dog out, as I didn't know what could happen. I laid back down in bed and I went to sleep! I didn't awake until the next morning 8:30 a.m.; seven hours?

I called the police a week or so later. They just told me to go to the ER or to call the Crisis center. Then they wrote down the telephone number of the Crisis center, and they left my home. About a week later I went to my church, the priest didn't believe me, or didn't want to discuss this encounter! I have never believed in UFOs or paranormal sightings, or have I ever viewed any website on my computer until after I encountered these two strange people looking in to my bedroom window.

This was not a dream! I was completely awake! No medicine I take has any side effects that would cause me to hallucinate! I am a senior citizen and I am living alone. This has scared me. They have not come back! I worry that they might come back. I have so many questions. I also called Channel 113 EWTN-TV. The person I talked to at EWTN didn't believe me and did not want to discuss the matter. Please e-mail me. I have not told my friends or family. Please help me with questions I have. I pray daily that I never see them again." Name Withheld

I called the witness and received more specific details, though most of it was personal. She did state that these beings wore full-length cloaks that were the same color (grayish-brown) of the cone-like covering over the head and face. The cone was more like a helmet. She also stated that she never sleeps more than three hours without waking, but she slept for an uninterrupted seven hours, which she states she has never done before or since.

After receiving the additional details, I came up with one possibility. In some respects, these beings remind me of the descriptions for the 'Teros' species, a supposed Earth underground dwelling race of humanoids with cone-shaped heads. They do have human-like facial features, so this may have been a face covering of some type. They are also referred to as 'Sunaynans' ('The Yearly Ones') an ancient race that appears at a certain time of the year. Some of the early native people of North America mentioned them; mostly in the desert Southwest. So, this sighting does kind of parallel the legends since this occurred in Arizona.

IN DIFFICULT CASES, I will sometimes ask my colleague and friend Deleece Cook to get involved. Along with her group (APPI– Australian Paranormal Phenomenon Investigators), Deleece conducted a remote view session on the Surprise, Arizona encounter and released the findings below:

Remote Viewing Session – Phantoms & Monsters

Ref. Surprise, Arizona, 2015. REMOTE VIEWING SESSION

Viewer: Deleece Cook Date: April 2016

CASE: Phantoms & Monsters Session for: LON STRICKLER Report Date: February 10, 2016

Date of Occurrence: Days prior to Christmas 2015 Location: Surprise, Phoenix, Arizona USA Latitude: 33.629234, Longitude: -112.367928

GPS: 33° 37' 45.2424" N - 112° 22' 4.5408" W

RV Impressions: I am focusing upon the beings that were described in the case. My RV & psychic impressions are recorded below – the 'Message' are the words given to me. The 'Interpretation' is the expansion of the message:

The emotional dialogue I receive. There were 3 windows open:

I think this relates to three portals.

- One of the portals is damaged

- A building with a broken window or entrance.

There were three identities (figures) originally: One of the identities is hurt or/and missing.

There is a deep sense of separation about this situation. There is a deep sense of abandonment.

There is a deep sense of disconnection.

A search is in progress – they are searching for something, and they are being searched for.

The seeking of sanctuary:

Outcasts and Refugees – Workers - slaves unsure of what to do in their situation.

Male Energy:

They are male energized. They have a sense of self.

They are related but not the same.

They have a sense of what being afraid is - maybe it's more a sense of being unsure – this is not a familiar feeling they are experiencing.

A change in the Hierarchy:

A power challenge and a change in their previous environmental civilizational structure – new rules – aggressive searching – new duties to perform without instruction.

Unknown territory:

Out of their natural environment - New lands and new opportunities. They are pioneers - they are trying to leave. They are having trouble adjusting to a new place.

They came to look for one thing – but they are looking for another:

There is a very important aspect here – the 'Very Important Purpose' that they are supposed to be looking for is not what they *are doing when the lady saw them. I will explain the VIP in a diagram (below) – this is new ground. They are in a 'predicament' which I think has been outlined above – they are lost/unsure and are looking for food – but I think food means medicine in this case.*

They are not in the place they are supposed to be:

They are out of their realm – yet they persist because they are 'programmed'(?) to proceed – but they do not know how to exactly – they think/know they are in the wrong location – but they investigate for their needs – orders.

They are members of a team:

They are doing their part to play in this bigger agenda – but their part is important. There is more than one team trying to do the same thing. There is a race mentality here – both a 'competition' and a 'species' race.

Evolution ascended/ascending:

Advanced beings? Evolved beings? This may have more to do with the VIP drawing/diagram. I get the words "Higher Codes."

Impotent:

These Identities were not a danger.

ReDNA:

There is a very strong sense here that tells me of a code or a classification called 'RED DNA' or 'ReDNA' or 'R.E.DNA' – it is not known of.

There seems to be some form of research going on with this REDNA/ReDNA/R.E.DNA but it is done in secret and maybe done in an underground scientific facility.

It does not seem to be originally from this planet, but it is now (if that makes sense).

It takes the form of a type of sequence similar to a chemical algorithm.

I have drawn it for you – though I have no idea if what I saw is the actual sequence or if it is just a close impression of what it looks like scientifically – or maybe some genome map.

Something about the two entities tells me that they have unwittingly given up this information (they know no better). The information is not important to them, nor do they know the relevance of it.

I see a man (human) working on this ReDNA/Red DNA/ R.E.DNA – dark hair, white coat though he looks as if he is from the era of the 50's/60's/70's.

This research may be from back then – but it is now very prevalent for some reason – I think it's 'discovery' is trying to be manipulated for weaponry – but it has more to do with human body and comes from it or is entwined within it.

The words I get are:

Rare – Pure – Astounding – recalcitrant (meaning it has its own will? Or they are finding it hard to control or manipulate further – maybe it refuses to be changed by its own will –maybe it is the 'will') Further note on the ReDNA/Red DNA/R.E.DNA:

I Googled the words and there are some pages regarding genetics – though it is out of my realm, none specifically called it RED DNA or ReDNA or R.E.DNA.

The pages I saw also showed some type of protein binders – some of the examples related to insulins and I wondered if the woman has a history of diabetes or blood sugar or is insulin intolerant (or something like that).

The picture of the sequence was very clear, and I have drawn it for you (above).

To add:

I also see a corporate building – top floor – lots of glass windows – windy outside – afternoon – a young man is in the open- plan office looking at a computer screen constantly checking it for updates – he seems agitated and impatient. He is in daytime, what he is looking at and checking on (on) the screen is in night time. He is wearing a white shirt, pants, a nice belt. He reminds me of the scientist from the 50's/60's/70's that was mentioned above. I'm not sure if this young man is related to the scientist or is actually the same person (time manipulation) they look very similar. There are others in the office working, both men and women. It is a large corporation but only has 11 workers in it – they are human.

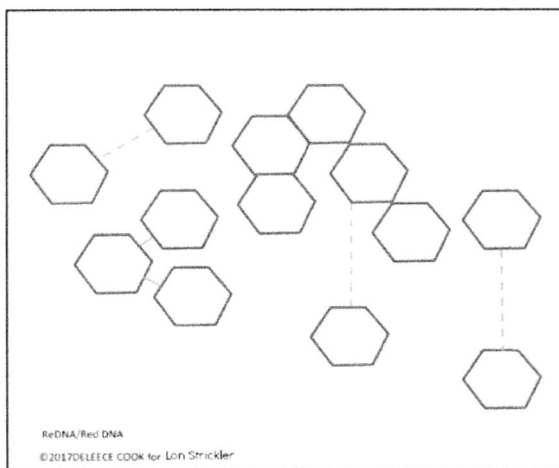

ReDNA/Red DNA
©2017DELEECE COOK for Lon Strickler

The sequence:
This is what I saw – in these colours I have drawn it in.

231

The other thing was this sequence was overlaid on the top of a piece of granite or polished grey rock – like a casket top.

The Witness:

(Personal information redacted in order to maintain privacy)

NDE - OBE: There was something that happened that night to the woman/person beyond just seeing the identities. I am not sure the person believes that they saw this – like it's not real? Metabolic imbalances and high rates of pulses.

APPI – Australian Paranormal Phenomenon Investigators.

I am grateful to Deleece for conducting this session. She was not provided with any background information, other than what was included in the original post. This is why I was not involved with the RV session.

Much of her interpretation on the witness was spot on. I also suspected a possible OBE.

If you remember some of the information from David Eckhart's case, he described various humanoids / alien entities (including humans) being used as slave labor in massive underground caverns located on Earth. As well, many of these humans were used in experimental capacities, as observed by David at another facility he was taken to by his non-human (Reptilian) handler during an abduction. Is it possible that these particular humanoids were escaped 'slaves' who accessed a 'portal,' and eventually made their way to the surface?

The scientific human interaction may also be a link to D.U.M.B. (Deep Underground Military Bases) laboratories and/or joint (alien and human) facilities theorized to exist throughout the world.

13

A MESSAGE...AND THE MESSENGERS

SINCE JUNE 20, 2010, I have be researching an email that was circulated worldwide. In a span of three days (June 17-20, 2010) hundreds, if not thousands, of experiencers, researchers and enthusiasts received an anonymous message through their email that supposedly originated from a location in Mississippi. There was no email address or return link in the syntax, but there was an ISP that indicated that the sender was in Mississippi at the time the emails were sent.

The text of the various emails was somewhat different, and it was sent using several languages. There was also at least one email that included several strange bits of code. As far as I know, that particular email was only partially deciphered. A few individuals claimed that they received the message by telephone and on shortwave radio, though I cannot verify this.

Over time, I collected the various versions received including those emails that were translated into English. The following narrative is a conglomeration of the message:

CHANGE THE WORLD! DECIDE WHETHER WE SHOULD SHOW UP!

"Whoever transmitted this translated message to you is irrelevant and should remain anonymous in your mind. It is what you will do with this message which matters. Each one of you wishes to exercise her / his free will and experience happiness. These are attributes that were shown to us and to which we now have access. Your free will depends upon the knowledge you have of your own power. Your happiness depends upon the love that you give and receive. Like all conscious races at this stage of progress, you may feel isolated on your planet. This impression makes you sure of your destiny. Yet, you are at the brink of big upheavals that only a minority is aware of. It is not our responsibility to modify your future without you choosing it. Consider this message as a worldwide referendum. And your answer as a ballot. Who are we?

Neither your scientists nor your religious representatives speak unanimously about the unexplained celestial events that mankind has witnessed for thousands of years. To know the truth, one must face it without the filter of one's beliefs, however respectable they may be.

A growing number of your anonymous researchers are exploring new knowledge paths and are getting very close to reality. Today, your civilization is flooded with an ocean of information of which only a tiny part, the less upsetting one, is notably diffused. In the past fifty years, what seemed ridiculous or improbable has often become possible. Be aware that the future will be even more surprising. You will discover the worst as well as the best.

Like billions of other beings in this galaxy, we are conscious creatures that some have named 'extra-terrestrials,' even though reality is subtler. There is no fundamental difference between you and us, save for the experience of certain stages of evolution. Like in any other organized *structure, hierarchy exists in our internal relationships. Ours is based upon the wisdom of several races. It is with the approval of this hierarchy that we turn to you. Like most of you, we are in the quest of the Supreme Being. Therefore, we are not gods or lesser gods but virtually your equals in the Cosmic Brotherhood. Physically, we are somewhat different from you but most of us are 'humanoid-shaped.'*

Our existence is a reality but the majority of you do not perceive it yet. We are not mere observers. We have consciences just like you. You fail to apprehend us because we remain invisible to your senses and measuring instruments most of the time. We wish to fill this void at this moment in your history. We made this collective decision, but this is not enough. We need yours. Through this message, you become the decision-makers. You personally. We have no human representative on Earth who could guide your decision. Why aren't we visible?

At certain stages of evolution, cosmic 'humanities' discover new forms of science beyond the apparent control of matter. Structured dematerialization and materialization are part of them. This is what your humanity has reached in a few laboratories, in close collaboration with other extra-terrestrial creatures at the cost of hazardous compromises that remain purposely hidden from you by some of your representatives.

Apart from the aerial or spatial objects or phenomena known by your scientific community, that you call 'UFOs,' there are essentially multidimensional manufactured ships that apply these capacities.

Many human beings have been in visual, auditory, tactile or psychic contact with such ships, some of which are under occult powers that govern you. The scarcity of your observations is due to the outstanding advantages provided by the dematerialized state of these ships. By not witnessing them by yourself, you cannot believe in their existence. We fully understand this.

The majority of these observations are made on an individual basis so as to touch the soul and not to modify any organized system. This is deliberate from the races that surround you but for very different reasons and results. For negative multidimensional beings that play a part in the exercise of power in the shadow of human oligarchy, discretion is motivated by their will to keep their existence and seizure unknown. For us, discretion is motivated by the respect of the human free will that people can exercise to manage their own affairs so that they can reach technical and spiritual maturity on their own.

Humankind's entrance into the family of galactic civilizations is greatly expected. We can appear in broad daylight and help you attain this union. We haven't done it so far, as too few of you have genuinely desired it, because of ignorance, indifference or fear, and because the emergency of the situation did not justify it. Many of those who study our appearances count the lights in the night without lighting the way. Often, they think in terms of objects when it is all about conscious beings. Who are you?

You are the offspring of many traditions that throughout time have been mutually enriched by each's contributions. The same applies to the races under the surface of the Earth. Your goal is to unite in the respect of these roots to accomplish a common project. The appearance of your cultures seems to keep you separated because you substitute it to your deeper being. Shape is now more important than the essence of your subtle nature. For the powers in place, this prevalence of the shape constitutes the ramparts against any form of jeopardy.

You are being called on to overcome shape while still respecting it for its richness and beauty. Understanding the *conscience of shape makes us love men in their diversity. Peace does not mean not making war, it consists in becoming what you are in reality: a same Fraternity. To understand this, the number of solutions within your reach are decreasing. One of them consists in contact with another race that would reflect the image of what you are in reality.*

What is your situation? Except for rare occasions, our interventions always had very little incidence on your capacity to make collective and individual decisions about your own future. This is motivated by our knowledge of your deep psychological mechanisms. We reached the conclusion that freedom is built every day as a being becomes aware of himself and of his environment, getting progressively rid of constraints and inertias, whatever they may be. Despite the numerous, brave and willing human consciences, those inertias are artificially maintained for the profit of a growing centralizing power.

Until recently, mankind lived a satisfying control of its decisions. But it is losing more and more the control of its own fate because of the growing use of advanced technologies, which lethal consequences on the Earthly and human ecosystems become irreversible. You are slowly but surely losing your extraordinary capacity to make life desirable. Your resilience will artificially decrease, independently of your own will. Such technologies exist that affect your body as well as your mind. Such plans are on their way. This can change as long as you keep this creative power in you, even if it cohabits with the dark intentions of your potential lords. This is the reason why we remain invisible. This individual power is doomed to vanish should a collective reaction of great magnitude not happen. The period to come is that of rupture, whichever it may be.

But should you wait for the last moment to find solutions?

Should you anticipate or undergo pain? Your history has never ceased to be marked by encounters between peoples who had to discover one another in conditions that were often conflictual. Conquests almost always happened to the detriment of others. Earth has now become a village where everyone knows everyone else. But still, conflicts continue to persist, and threats of all kinds get worse in duration and intensity. Although a human being as an individual, yet having many potential capacities, cannot exercise them with dignity. This is the case for the biggest majority of you for reasons that are essentially geopolitical. There are several billion of you. The education of your children and your living conditions, as well as the conditions of numerous animals and much plant life are nevertheless under the thumb of a small number of your political, financial, military and religious representatives.

Your thoughts and beliefs are modeled after partisan interests to turn you into slaves while at the same time giving you the feeling that you are in total control of your destiny, which in essence is the reality. But there is a long way between a wish and a fact when the true rules of the game at hand are unknown. This time, you are not the conqueror. Biasing information is a millenary strategy for human beings. Inducting thoughts, emotions or organisms that do not belong to you via ad hoc technologies is an even older strategy. Wonderful opportunities of progress stand close to big subdual and destruction threats. These dangers and opportunities exist now. However, you can only perceive what is being shown to you. The end of natural resources is programmed whereas no long-term collective project has been launched. Ecosystem exhaustion mechanisms have exceeded irreversible limits. The scarcity of resources and their unfair distribution - resources which entry price will rise day after day - will bring about fratricide fights at a large scale, but also at the very heart of your cities and country sides.

Hatred grows bigger but so does love. That is what keeps you confident in your ability to find solutions. But the critical mass is insufficient, and sabotage work is cleverly being carried out. Human behaviors, formed from past habits and trainings, have such an inertia that this perspective leads you to a dead end. You entrust these problems to representatives, whose conscience of common well- being slowly fades away in front of corporatist interests, with those difficulties. They are always debating on the form but rarely on the content. Just at the moment of action, delays will accumulate to the point when you have to submit rather than choose.

This is the reason why, more than ever in your history, your decisions of today will directly and significantly impact your survival of tomorrow. What event could radically modify this inertia that is typical of any civilization? Where will a collective and unifying awareness come from, that will stop this blind rushing ahead? Tribes, populations and human nations have always encountered and 189 interacted with one another. Faced with the threats weighing upon the human family, it is perhaps time that a greater interaction occurred. A great roller wave is on the verge of emerging. It mixes very positive but also very negative aspects.

Who are the 'third party?" There are two ways to establish a cosmic contact with another civilization: via its standing representatives or directly with individuals without distinction. The first way entails the struggle for interests. The second way brings awareness. The first way was chosen by a group of races motivated by keeping mankind in slavery, thereby controlling Earth resources, the gene pool and human emotional energy. The second way was chosen by a group of races allied with the cause of the spirit of service. We have, at our end, subscribed to this disinterested cause and introduced ourselves a few years ago to representatives of the human power who refused our outstretched hand on the pretext of incompatible interests with their strategic vision. That is why today individuals are to make this choice by themselves without any representative interfering. What we proposed in the past to those whom we believed were in a capacity to contribute to your happiness, we propose it now to you!

Most of you ignore that non-human creatures took part in the exercise of those centralizing powers without them being neither suspected nor accessible to your senses. This is so true that they have almost very subtly taken control. They do not necessarily stand on your material plane, and that is precisely what could make them extremely efficient and frightening in the near future. However, be aware that a large number of your representatives are fighting this danger. Be aware that not all abductions are made against you. It is difficult to recognize the truth! How could you under such conditions exercise your free will when it is so much manipulated? What are you really free of?

Peace and reunification of your peoples would be a first step toward the harmony with civilizations other than yours. That is precisely what those who manipulate you behind the scenes want to avoid at all cost because, by dividing, they reign. They also reign over those who govern you. Their strength comes from their capacity to distillate mistrust and fear into you. This considerably harms your very cosmic nature. This message would be of no interest if these manipulators' tutorate did not reach its peak and if their misleading and murderous plans did not materialize in a few years from now. Their deadlines are close, and mankind will undergo unprecedented torments for the next ten cycles. To defend yourselves against this aggression that bears no face, *you need at least to have enough information that leads to the solution. As is also the case with humans, resistance exists amongst those dominant races. Here again, appearance will not be enough to tell the dominator from the ally. At your current state of psychism, it is extremely difficult for you to distinguish between them. In addition to your intuition, training will be necessary when the time has come. Being aware of the priceless value of free will, we are inviting you to an alternative. What can we offer?*

We can offer you a more holistic vision of the universe and of life, constructive interactions, the experience of fair and fraternal relationships, liberating technical knowledge, eradication of suffering, controlled exercise of individual powers, the access to new forms of energy and, finally, a better comprehension of consciousness.

We cannot help you overcome your individual and collective fears, or bring you laws that you would not have chosen, work on your own selves, individual and collective effort to build the world you desire, the spirit of quest to new skies. What would we receive? Should you decide that such a contact takes place, we would rejoice over the safeguarding of fraternal equilibrium in this region of the universe, fruitful diplomatic exchanges, and the intense joy of knowing that you are united to accomplish what you are capable of. The feeling of joy is strongly sought in the universe for its energy is divine. What is the question we ask you?

DO YOU WISH THAT WE SHOW UP?

How can you answer this question? The truth of soul can be read by telepathy. You only need to clearly ask yourself this question and give your answer as clearly, on your own or in a group, as you wish. Being in the heart of a city or in the middle of a desert does not impact the efficiency of your answer, YES or NO, IMMEDIATELY AFTER ASKING THE

QUESTION! Just do it as if you were speaking to yourself but thinking about the message. This is a universal question and these mere few words, put in their context, have a powerful meaning. You should not let hesitation in the way. This is why you 191 should calmly think about it, in all conscience. In order to perfectly associate your answer with the question, it is recommended that you answer right after another reading of this message. Do not rush to answer. Breathe and let all the power of your own free will penetrate you. Be proud of what you are! The problems that you may have weaken you. Forget about them for a few minutes to be yourselves. Feel the force that springs up in you. You are in control of yourselves! A single thought, a single answer can drastically change your near future, in one way as in another. Your individual decision of asking in your inner self that we show up on your material plan and in broad daylight is precious and essential to us. Even though you can choose the way that best suits you, rituals are essentially useless. A sincere request made with your heart on your own will always be perceived by those of us whom it is sent to. In your own private polling booth of your secret will, you will determine the future. What is the lever effect?

This decision should be made by the greatest number among you, even though it might seem like a minority. It is recommended to spread this message, in all envisioned fashions, in as many languages as possible, to those around you, whether or not they seem receptive to this new vision of the future. You can even openly and publicly make fun of it if it makes you feel more comfortable. but do not be indifferent for at least you will have exercised your free will. Forget about the false prophets and the beliefs that have been transmitted to you about us. This request is one of the most intimate that can be asked to you. Deciding by yourself, as an individual, is your *right as well as your responsibility! Passivity only leads to the absence of freedom.*

Similarly, indecision is never efficient. If you really want to cling to your beliefs, which is something that we understand, then say NO. If you do not know what to choose, do not say YES because of mere curiosity. This is not a show, this is real daily life, WE ARE ALIVE! And living!

Your history has plenty of episodes when determined men and women were able to influence the thread of events in spite of their small number. Just like a small number is enough to take temporal power on Earth and influence the future of the majority, a small number of you can radically change your fate as an answer to the impotence in face of so much inertia and hurdles! You can ease mankind's birth to brotherhood. One of your thinkers once said: "Give me a hand-hold and I'll raise the Earth." Spreading this message will then be the hand-hold to strengthen, we will be the light-years long lever, you will be the craftsmen to raise the Earth as a consequence of our appearance. What would be the consequences of a positive decision?

For us, the immediate consequence of a collective favorable decision would be the materialization of many ships, in your sky and on Earth.

For you, the direct effect would be the rapid abandoning of many certitudes and beliefs. A simple conclusive visual contact would have huge repercussions on your future. Much knowledge would be modified forever. The organization of your societies would be deeply upheaved forever, in all fields of activity. Power would become individual because you would see for yourself that we are living. Concretely, you would change the scale of your values! The most important thing for us is that humankind would form a single family in front of this "unknown" we would represent! Danger would slowly melt away from your homes because you would indirectly force the undesirable ones, those we name the 'third party,' to show up and vanish. You would all bear the same name and share the same roots: Mankind!

Later on, peaceful and respectful exchanges would be thus possible if such is your wish. For now, he who is hungry cannot smile, he who is fearful cannot welcome us. We are sad to see men, women and children suffering to such a degree in their flesh and in their hearts when they bear such an inner light. This light can be your future. Our relationships could be progressive. Several stages of several years or decades would occur, demonstrative appearance of our ships, physical appearance beside human beings, collaboration in your technical and spiritual evolution, discovery of parts of the galaxy.

Every time, new choices would be offered to you. You would then decide by yourself to cross new stages if you think it necessary to your external and inner well-being. No interference would be decided upon unilaterally. We would leave as soon as you would collectively wish that we do. Depending upon the speed to spread the message 193 across the world, several weeks, or even several months will be necessary before our 'great appearance,' if such is the decision made by the majority of those who will have used their capacity to choose, and if this message receives the necessary support. The main difference between your daily prayers to entities of a strictly spiritual nature and your current decision is extremely simple: we are technically equipped to materialize. Why such a historical dilemma?

We know that 'foreigners' are considered as enemies as long as they embody the 'unknown.' In a first stage, the emotion that our appearance will generate will strengthen your relationships on a worldwide scale. How could you know *whether our arrival is the consequence of your collective choice? For the simple reason that we would have otherwise been already there for a long time at your level of existence! If we are not there yet, it is because you have not made such a decision explicitly. Some among you might think that we would make you believe in a deliberate choice of yours so as to legitimate our arrival, though this would not be true. What interest would we have to openly offer you what you haven't got any access to yet, for the benefit of the greatest number of you?*

How could you be certain that this is not yet another subtle maneuver of the 'third party' to better enslave you? Because one always more efficiently fights something that is identified than the contrary. Isn't the terrorism that corrodes you a blatant example? Whatever, you are the sole judge in your own heart and soul. Whatever your choice, it would be respectable and respected. In the absence of human representatives who could potentially seduce into error you ignore everything about us as well as from about those who manipulate you without your consent. In your situation, the precautionary principle that consists in not trying to discover us does no longer prevail. You are already in the Pandora's box that the 'third party' has created around you. Whatever your decision may be, you will have to get out of it. In the face of such a dilemma, one ignorance against another, you need to ask your intuition. Do you want to see us with your own eyes, or simply believe what your thinkers say? That is the real question!

After thousands of years, one day, this choice was going to be inevitable: choosing between two unknowns. Why spread such a message among yourselves?

Translate and spread this message widely. This action will affect your future in an irreversible and historical way at the scale of millenniums, otherwise, it will postpone a new opportunity to choose to several years later, at least one generation, if it can survive. Not choosing stands for undergoing other's choices. Not informing other's stands for running the risk of obtaining a result that is contrary to one's expectations. Remaining indifferent means giving up one's free will.

It is all about your future. It is all about your evolution.

It is possible that this invitation does not receive your collective assent and that, because of a lack of information, it will be disregarded. Nevertheless, no individual desire goes unheeded in the universe. Imagine our arrival tomorrow. Thousands of ships. A unique cultural shock in today's mankind history. It will then be too late to regret about not making a choice and spreading the message because this discovery will be irreversible. We do insist that you do not rush into it but do think about it. And decide! The media will not be necessarily interested in spreading this message. It is therefore your task, as an anonymous yet an extraordinary thinking and loving being, to transmit it. You are still the architects of your own fate."

I also received a copy of this 'manifesto' in my email, though the person who supposedly forwarded it to me denies that they did so. Let's say that this was an actual message from another non-human group or race. Apart from it seeming like a threat, there are some statements within it that offer truth and reality. As well, since the narrative was disseminated about 9 years ago, it is possible that some of the detailed actions may have already occurred.

Once again, the circumstances in which this email was distributed does make its origin questionable. I believe that it may be safe to assume that, despite its authenticity, there does seem to be a definite agenda being outlined. I suppose it's just a matter of believing if our future could develop as described.

So, who are these messengers? Are these the benevolent galactic watchers, as described in the message, who really have our interests in mind? Experiencers receive directives from various sources. Most are benign, but on some occasions the information is profound and the messenger itself is surprising.

There was a period of time, for approximately a year or so, that I began to notice different species of owls around me. It didn't matter where I was during the evening, I would either see or hear an owl. During the daytime, I would constantly see pictures of owls or read a reference pertaining to one. It was occurring so often that I began to tell the people around me about it. I would also mention it on social media.

Not long after this phenomenon began, my wife was diagnosed with colon cancer. I didn't associate the owls with my wife's illness, but as time went on, I began to realize that I was being given a warning. As my wife's condition grew worse, I was noticing a higher number of owl sightings.

The evening before she passed away, a large barn owl perched itself on a tree branch outside of my apartment. My son and I had just returned home from the hospital, knowing that she was on death's door. The owl remained on the branch for about an hour. I heard one final 'hoot' as it flew away. 10 minutes later I received a call from the ICU, letting me know that my wife had just died.

About a month later, my 103-year-old grandmother, who was terminally ill in a nursing home in Gettysburg, had passed away. The day of the funeral, I was talking to my father when he mentioned an owl in the English Walnut tree the night my grandmother passed. He said that the owl kept him awake the entire night. We had never seen an owl around the property, but one decided to show up that particular night.

Since that time, I have talked to several paranormal researchers about my owl encounters. About the same time, experiencer Mike Clelland had released his book, "The Messengers: Owls, Synchronicity and the UFO Abductee." His preface stated:

"The owl has held a place of reverence and mystique throughout history. And as strange as this might seem, owls are also showing up in conjunction with the UFO experience. The author has collected a wealth of first-hand accounts in which owls manifest in the highly charged moments that surround alien contact. There is a strangeness to these accounts that defy simple explanations. This book explores implications that go far beyond what more conservative researchers would dare consider. But the owl connection encompasses more than the UFO experience. It also includes profound synchronicities, ancient archetypes, dreams, shamanistic experiences, personal transformation, and death. From the mythic legends of our ancient past to the first-hand accounts of the UFO abductee, owls are playing some vital role. This is also a deeply personal story. It is an odyssey of self-discovery as the author grapples with his own owl and UFO encounters. What plays out is a story of transformation with the owl at the heart of this journey."

I read the book and was totally floored. I had to speak to Mike, and I would soon have the opportunity to do so on our radio show. But this was just one type of messenger. Are the alien races using other physical beings from our planet in order to get their warnings and agenda distributed to the humans? Could these messages actually be from a collective consciousness?

I had a conversation with a fairly well-known remote viewer

who stated that they have contacted various alien races, during different sessions, and have received messages by means of 'automatic writing.' As well, some occult and paranormal enthusiast confirm that they have received actual extraterrestrial communication by using divination tools and techniques. Some of these revelations may seem a bit offbeat and divergent, but I would never discount their testimony out of hand.

Then there are the experiencers who confront these beings through abduction or during a close encounter. Science contends that the idea of making contact and communicating with aliens is a mainstay of science fiction. It is quite possible that an alien civilization has tried contacting us, but we simply didn't understand what they were conveying. I believe that it's reasonable to assume that any communication between aliens and humans, at this point in history, would depend on the aliens having knowledge of at least one human language.

Most experiencers that I have researched state that personal communication with extraterrestrials is achieved through an extra-sensory mechanism using human language. In other instances, the experiencer was shown written text, sometimes accompanied by images and sounds. I have also been told by a few experiencers that they heard audible words coming from an unknown source.

I can't say if there is a specific alien civilization responsible for the majority of these messages but, for the most part, I believe that there are factions that include several different races. I also believe that evolved and hybrid humans are part of at least one of the allied groups.

Do any of these factions possess a kindred connection with mankind? I doubt that their sentiments are akin to the feelings demonstrated in the film E.T.: The Extraterrestrial; but I also doubt that reality is comparable to War of the Worlds either.

It has become apparent that some alien races can demonstrate a modicum of benevolence towards humans, while others express little tolerance for our species. Experiencers have expressed a common theme when it comes to the alien beings they have encountered. There is a hierarchy with no dissension among them and that they have an accepted concept. That concept is that humans are a lesser species that will be employed in any manner the agenda calls for.

I stated in the introduction of this book:

"Why are these alien beings so concerned with Earth and its dominant human species? The most straightforward answer to that question is that we retain a connection to them."

"Our history is intertwined with extraterrestrial beings. I truly believe that humans are a genetic extension of otherworldly races. I also believe that most of the alien entities that people encounter are biologically enhanced and evolved humans from our past and future. But we must always keep in mind; they do have an agenda. I believe that agenda is eventual technological and biological singularity."

They made us. They need us. Humans are the experiment that went well. We are an insurance policy that can be used over and over. They are our Gods, and we are theirs for any means necessary.

ABOUT THE AUTHOR

Lon Strickler is a Fortean researcher, author, and publisher of the syndicated 'Phantoms and Monsters' blog. He began the blog in 2005, which has steadily grown in popularity and is read daily by tens of thousands of paranormal enthusiasts, investigators and those seeking the truth. His research and reports have been featured on hundreds of online media sources. Several of these published reports have been presented on various television segments, including The History Channel's 'Ancient Aliens,' Syfy's 'Paranormal Witness', 'Fact or Faked: Paranormal

Files,' and Destination America's 'Monsters and Mysteries in America.'

He has been interviewed on hundreds of radio & online broadcasts, including multiple guest appearances on 'Coast to Coast AM.' He was also featured on Destination America's 'Monsters and Mysteries in America' television show for 'The Sykesville Monster' episode. Lon has written 8 books and is currently the host of Arcane Radio on Beyond Explanation YouTube channel.

Lon was born and raised in south central Pennsylvania, near the Gettysburg National Military Park and Battlefield. After living in the Baltimore, MD metro area for 40 years, he eventually moved back to his hometown in 2016.

Printed in Great Britain
by Amazon